Railway Memor

BARNSL
CUDWORTH &
ROYSTON

DAVID GREEN & PETER ROSE

BELLCODE BOOKS
10 RIDGE BANK TODMORDEN
WEST YORKSHIRE OL14 7BA

ISBN 1 871233 07 0

Edited by Stephen Chapman

Printed by the Amadeus Press Ltd., Huddersfield.

ABOVE: On 12th October, 1962 the Hull and Barnsley lower quadrant home signal at Cudworth Yard South Junction was replaced by the standard BR upper quadrant type behind it. The signal fitters prepare the old signal for removal as Mexborough WD 2-8-0 No. 90384 brings a load of coal off the Stairfoot line. *(Peter Rose)*

FRONT COVER: Beautifully polished Holbeck Jubilee 4-6-0 No 45568 *Western Australia* and her clean coaches make a glorious sight while calling at Royston & Notton station with the 4.15pm Leeds City to Sheffield Midland stopping train on 30th May, 1962. *(Peter Rose)*

FRONTICEPIECE: Royston residents, 8F 2-8-0 No. 48113 and ex-Midland 3F 0-6-0 No. 43705 rest outside their shed on 9th May, 1954. *(J.C.Hillmer)*

BACK COVER TOP: Barnsley Court House station in the 1950s. Mexborough-based B1 4-6-0 No. 61194 rolls a Penistone to Doncaster local past regular Barnsley ex-Great Central C13 4-4-2T No. 67434. *(David Green)*

BACK COVER BOTTOM: The coal industry kept working steam alive around Barnsley long after it had been ousted from British Rail. Here a National Coal Board Austerity 0-6-0ST (Hunslet 2857 built 1943) marshals BR high capacity coal wagons at Dodworth Colliery on 28th December, 1971. Following withdrawal at Dodworth, this locomotive received a new lease of life at Cadley Hill Colliery in the Midlands. *(Adrian Booth)*

INTRODUCTION

To most people Barnsley means coal but Cudworth and Royston have less obvious connotations.

Many railway enthusiasts will remember that Royston had a locomotive depot which became the last in the West Riding to use steam. Historians will know that Cudworth marked the spot where the old Hull and Barnsley Railway's main line petered out, its bid to reach Barnsley thwarted by its rivals.

In fact, between these two villages a vast expanse of lines, junctions, marshalling yards, and two locomotive depots, clung to the London-Carlisle Midland main line for two and a half miles.

Within a space seven miles by eight was a tangled web of railways which proliferated during the 19th and early 20th centuries for shifting Barnsley coal to markets and ports as cheaply and efficiently as possible.

The different railway companies which sought the wealth created by the lucrative Barnsley seam brought a rich diversity of engines, rolling stock and infrastructure.

They ranged from the Midland main line with its long-distance expresses and endless procession of heavy goods trains to the humble colliery tracks which kept working steam alive into the 1980s. In **Railway Memories No.8** we turn the clock back to those days in the not too distant past when there were railways, collieries and coke works seemingly at the end of every field, when the Barnsley area required three locomotive depots, when railways criss-crossed each other on high viaducts and huge girder bridges, and when Barnsley had not one but two stations.

Publication of this book, means that the Railway Memories series now provides a continuous illustrated record of the traditional railway from the fringes of Sheffield to the foot of the Settle and Carlisle line.

CONTENTS

A wonderful scene summing up the Great Central influence around Barnsley. Class D11/1 'Large Director' 4-4-0s Nos. 62664 *Princess Mary* and 62662 *Prince of Wales* run into Exchange station with the Ian Allan 'Pennine Pullman' railtour on 12th May, 1956. The train travelled from London via Sheffield, Manchester and the L&Y main line. *(Kenneth Field)*

SETTING THE SCENE

As the 20th century draws to a close, there is little tangible evidence that the rolling countryside around Barnsley was once festooned with a dense and vibrant railway network.

In fact, it is hard to believe now that until only recently it was a world-renowned centre of coal mining.

The Barnsley coalfield which the railways grew to serve is to all intents and purposes extinct while only the basic threads of a once great railway system survive.

Mining and railways grew to tap the rich Barnsley seam, up to 10ft deep and so-called because it outcropped in the hills above Barnsley. Easily accessible and mined at least since the 15th century, it was especially good for coking and steam raising. Nearly every pit had its own coke ovens along with plants producing tar and chemicals. Other industries based on local minerals grew up too - iron, glass and bricks, for example.

The earliest railways were tramroads taking coal from collieries in the hills to the nearest canal or ironworks. Worked by man, horse or winding engine they included the two-mile Silkstone tramway and the Elsecar & Thorncliffe tramway.

They were slow, could only move relatively small amounts and Barnsley needed main line railways to meet the increasing demands of the industrial revolution.

With many companies vying for this business Barnsley's rail network came to possess a rich diversity of character, operation and motive power lasting well after it had been unified under British Railways.

First and most important was the Derby-Leeds line of Railway King George Hudson's North Midland Railway, opened on 1st July, 1840.

Part of his main line from Leeds and York to London, it avoided steep gradients and bypassed such apparently insignificent places as Wakefield, Barnsley and Sheffield!

The NMR missed Barnsley by four miles to the east so it set up a station at Cudworth, called that Barnsley instead and connected it to the town by horse omnibus.

Another station was opened 2.5 miles further north at Royston and the area between the two eventually filled up with marshalling yards handling vast amounts of coal traffic.

When the North Midland joined other companies to form the Midland Railway, its line through Cudworth became part of the Midland main line from London St. Pancras, the West Country and the Midlands to Yorkshire and Scotland.

Barnsley was plugged into the main line on 28th June, 1869 when the Midland opened its branch from Cudworth to the town through Monk Bretton, starting a regular passenger service on 2nd May, 1870. It became a push-pull train known locally as the 'Pusha' and was until the mid-1950s worked by 1880s 0-4-4 tank engines.

The first railway into Barnsley itself was the Sheffield, Rotherham, Barnsley, Wakefield, Huddersfield and Goole whose first section, from Barnsley to the Lancashire and Yorkshire Railway's Wakefield-Manchester main line at Horbury, opened for business in January, 1850 along with a 1.75-mile goods branch to Silkstone.

Coal traffic, especially to Goole docks, grew so fast that five years later the Horbury line had to be doubled, only 1,745-yard Woolley Tunnel staying single track until a second bore was added in 1902.

The second phase, opened on 4th September, 1854, ran south from Aldam Junction, Wath, to Meadow Hall, Sheffield. Serving Chapeltown and several collieries on the way, it began with a fierce 1 in 63 climb to Birdwell before descending like a helta-skelta towards Sheffield at 1 in 62. Barnsley-Sheffield trains had to reverse at Aldam Junction until 1879 when a new curve between New Oaks Junction(Stairfoot) and Wombwell Main allowed direct running.

The line north of Barnsley was leased to the L&Y before it opened and south of Barnsley to the South Yorkshire Railway which had already completed the Mexborough-Barnsley route through Aldam Junction in July, 1851.

The two companies shared the L&Y's single platform station in Barnsley, establishing a joint locomotive depot alongside.

Originally just Barnsley, the station became Barnsley Exchange in 1924. The Midland's original Barnsley station was renamed Cudworth in 1854.

For 110 years Barnsley Exchange had only one platform but it did boast a busy engine shed. Ex-Great Central 2-8-0 No. 63726, then class 04/5 with Gresley class O2 boiler, squeezes twixt shed and station while plodding along the old Sheffield, Rotherham, Barnsley, Wakefield, Huddersfield and Goole Railway with a coal train to Wath yard on 25th February, 1956. *(John F. Oxley)*

Pressure for a direct route to Manchester and Merseyside eventually persuaded the Manchester, Sheffield and Lincolnshire Railway, which swallowed up the South Yorkshire in 1874, to build the 6.75-mile connection up to its Manchester-Sheffield main line at Penistone. The steeply graded line took more than four years to complete, the first stage between Dodworth and Penistone opening for goods on 15th May, 1854. It was extended to Summer Lane by 5th December, 1855 and from there down a 1 in 50/41 gradient in almost continuous 50ft deep cutting to Barnsley Central goods station by February, 1857. Passenger trains ran between Summer Lane and Penistone from November, 1855 but did not reach Barnsley station until December, 1859.

By all accounts, the town's first station was a miserable place dubbed 'that beastly hole' by one observer. It embarrassed the MSL which joined the Midland in building a new station situated on higher ground immediately above the existing one. Utilising the town's old court house for a station building, it was named accordingley.

The new station's west exit joined the MSL Penistone line at Court House Junction while the east exit to Cudworth was carried on viaducts and a skew girder bridge over the Mexborough line.

A connection from the Cudworth branch at Barnsley West Junction to the Mexborough line at Quarry Junction enabled Doncaster-Penistone and Barnsley-Sheffield Victoria services to use Court House along with the Midland's Cudworth trains from June, 1870.

The next two railways on the scene bore remarkable similarities to each other, not least their aims of shifting coal directly to the Humber ports and the construction delays and difficulties they encountered.

Sandwiched between the L&Y and Midland lines, the no-nonsense Barnsley Coal Railway was meant to go from Stairfoot to Wakefield but met tough opposition in Parliament and progressed just 4.75 miles before running out of steam at Applehaigh, near Notton. Opened in January, 1870 it remained a goods branch until the MSL, encouraged by completion of its Doncaster-Wakefield joint line with the Great Northern Railway in 1866, took the project on.

It laid another 4.75 miles of double track to a triangular junction with the Doncaster-Wakefield line at Nostell which allowed goods and mineral trains direct access to the Humber as well as new marshalling yards at Ardsley, between Wakefield and Leeds. It included a one-mile curve from Oakwell into

Barnsley(Old Oaks Junction), connections to Wharncliffe Woodmoor Colliery, Barnsley gas works and, from 1896, the Barnsley Brewery maltings at Oakwell.

The whole route finally opened for goods on 1st August, 1882. A Barnsley Court House-Leeds Central passenger service started a month later serving Staincross, Notton & Royston, and Ryhill & Wintersett stations.

Its passenger trains lasted barely half a century but the BCR became a key Great Central(the MSL's name from 1899) route from Sheffield and Manchester to Leeds, carrying express goods trains to the end.

Besides its own main line, the Hull & Barnsley Railway wanted running powers over other companies' lines to both Barnsley stations, Sheffield and even to Manchester and Liverpool via Woodhead. But by the time the main line opened in July, 1885, after taking six years to build, the other companies had successfully blocked all H&B attempts at running powers.

The H&B's trains were destined to go little further than Cudworth where it set up marshalling yards, a large locomotive depot, and a passenger platform alongside the Midland station. It also laid connections to Wharncliffe Woodmoor and Monckton Main collieries.

Goods lines extended another three miles, over the Midland's main line and under its Barnsley branch, to the MSL at Stairfoot, the nearest the H&B ever got to Barnsley. It was connected to the Midland main line at Cudworth South and to the Barnsley branch by goods exchange sidings at Monk Bretton Junction.

From 1905 the Midland allowed the H&B to run a through passenger train between Hull, Cudworth and Sheffield.

The H&B acquired new 4-4-0s and comfortable bogie coaches for the service but it was killed off by wartime cutbacks in 1917 and Cudworth became the terminus again.

Despite its problems, the H&B did carry plenty of coal from pits around Barnsley to its docks at Hull while timber pit props from Scandanavia provided return loads.

In 1922 the H&B was swallowed up by its arch rival, the North Eastern ready for the 1923 grouping of all the independant companies into the `Big Four'. It became part of the London & North Eastern Railway along with the GC, the Midland and L&Y joining the rival London, Midland & Scottish.

By the mid-1880s, railways reached Barnsley from every direction but one of its most important and surviving routes was yet to come.

Intending to build a 4.5-mile single goods track from its Derby-Leeds main line near today's Meadow Hall Interchange, to Thorncliffe iron works at Chapeltown, the Midland decided to press on with a double track main line that would open up a second route from Sheffield to the north.

The 7.75-mile continuation from just outside the Thorncliffe works to Barnsley opened for goods in April, 1897, Barnsley Court House-

Until 1960, Court House was the main station in Barnsley. It took its name from the old court house which was adapted as the station building. The station has long since been swept away but the court house itself survives as a bar and restaurant.
This was how it looked in the 1950s.
(David Green)

Sheffield Midland passenger trains started running on 1st July, calling at Wombwell, Elsecar & Hoyland, Wentworth & Tankersley, and Chapeltown.

A 3.25-mile goods branch from Wombwell (Wharncliffe Branch Sidings) ran to Wharncliffe Silkstone pit and coke ovens, near Birdwell, serving Barrow and Rockingham collieries on the way.

Over the years, these lines served around 20 collieries and industrial concerns with opencast mining becoming a major source of traffic in the 1940s and 50s. The last colliery to be served was Skiers Spring, Wentworth, where rail traffic ended in September, 1975.

The 2.5-mile line from Monk Spring Junction, just outside Barnsley, to Cudworth station was added in September, 1899, completing the through route known as the Chapeltown Loop.

Despite a ruling 1 in 100 northbound gradient, it was a useful alternative to the main line, allowing express passenger and freight trains to avoid bottlenecks around Rotherham.

Major structures along the way included the 1,498-yard Tankersley Tunnel, between Chapeltown and Wentworth, a 200-yard viaduct at Elsecar across a valley carrying the Hoyland Silkstone Colliery tramway, lofty Swaithe Viaduct over Worsborough Dale, a 232-yard viaduct carrying the Monk Spring-Cudworth line over Stairfoot Junction, and 209-yard Ardsley Tunnel.

This and the opening of a 3.5-mile MSL branch from Stairfoot to Houghton Colliery in 1892, together with existing MSL and H&B lines, turned Stairfoot into a railway Spaghetti Junction.

Meanwhile, the Midland was also building its West Riding line, a new direct route from Royston Junction to the north via Bradford. It opened in 1905 having got no further than Dewsbury but through a junction with the L&Y main line at Thornhill it became a vital link for cross-Pennine coal.

Local passenger trains serving stations at Middlestown and Crigglestone never materialised either but the line was used from 1909 to 1946 by a Bradford-Sheffield express and in the 1920s and 30s by the Bradford Exchange - St.Pancras "Yorkshireman", plus summer Saturday trains until the 1960s.

Barnsley's rail network reached its peak in 1905 when the Dearne Valley Railway, promoted by a group of coal owners, was completed to serve big new pits at Houghton Main, Grimethorpe and all points to Doncaster.

The first section, opened in 1902, left the H&B at Brierley Junction, just east of Cudworth. It was joined at Shafton in 1905 by the L&Y's 8.25-mile Dearne Valley Junction line from Crofton, Wakefield.

It was operated by the L&Y and for the next 60 years coal was taken to Crofton yards for forwarding to Goole and the other side of the Pennines.

The line was doubled in 1912 and the L&Y began running a steam railmotor for passengers between Wakefield Kirkgate and Edlington(near Doncaster), with rudimentary halts of low sleeper platforms and old coach body waiting rooms at Ryhill, Great Houghton, Grimethorpe and other pit villages further east. The service was fairly well patronised between Grimethorpe and Wakefield, lasting into BR days. The railmotors were replaced by ex-L&Y 2-4-2Ts and push-pull coaches by the second world war, and the 2-4-2Ts by new Ivatt 2-6-2Ts 41283 and 41284 shortly after the war.

The railways around Barnsley must have moved millions upon millions of tons of coal and coke from the pits and coking works which covered the landscape.

Trip workings ran day and night from local collieries to the yards at Wath, Carlton and Cudworth, or Healey Mills, Mirfield and Mytholmroyd in the Calder Valley. From there the coal continued across the Pennines, to the docks at Hull, Goole and Immingham, to the Midlands, London and the North West.

Traffic was so heavy that between 1923 and 1925 the LMS had to open out the 684-yard Chevet Tunnel, north of Royston, into a 100ft deep cutting so that it could quadruple the Midland main line. Then it built, brand new on virgin land, Royston motive power depot complete with a housing estate for its staff.

Around Barnsley itself, engines of LNER and GC origin predominated with GC 0-8-0s, 2-8-0s, 0-6-0s and 0-6-2Ts working goods trains and colliery trips. Dodging between them were local passenger trains of old wooden coaches bustled up and down to Penistone, Doncaster and Sheffield by elegant GC Atlantic tanks or 0-6-0s. Bigger 4-4-0s and 4-6-0s stormed the bank up to

Penistone with the few longer-distance workings like those from Cleethorpes or the evening fish trains from Hull to Guide Bridge and Grimsby to Ashton Moss, Manchester.

The L&Y 2-4-2Ts came down to Exchange with shuttles from Wakefield and in the 1950s took a turn on the Court House-Cudworth, and Sheffield Midland lines before being superseded by more recent engines, diesels or closure.

The 1950s Sheffield Midland service included the `sandwich' trains, push-pull units with the tank engine in the middle, as well as longer trains worked by Midland 4-4-0s or LMS 2-6-0s. Its premier trains of the 1960s were the Halifax portion of a Sheffield-St. Pancras express and the summer Saturday Bradford-Poole.

On the main line through Cudworth, Jubilees and the odd BR Britannia Pacific sped expresses like the "Thames-Clyde" past workaday 2-8-0s and 0-6-0s plodding in and out of Carlton yards. Long-distant freight trains, running mostly at night, linked London, Bristol, Birmingham, Leicester and Nottingham with Leeds, Carlisle, and Glasgow.

Mineral trains fed in from the Hull and Barnsley which in its heyday brought its own 0-6-0s and 0-8-0s. Following the grouping, these gradually gave way to GC 2-8-0s and ex-NER types like the Q5 0-8-0s, until under BR the route became, like the Dearne Valley, dominated by 8F and WD 2-8-0s.

The H&B's passenger trains must have been a real treat with their blue domeless 2-4-0s and 4-4-0s arriving at Cudworth alongside the Midland's red 2-4-0s, 4-4-0s and 4-2-2s.

Just 25 years after the network reached its peak, depression, recession, bus competition, rationalisation, and amalgamations bringing duplicate lines under one owner, combined to fuel a gradually accelerating decline.

Barnsley Court House-Leeds trains over the Coal Railway were the first casualty, axed by the LNER on 22nd September, 1930, leaving Barnsley with virtually no through trains to Leeds for the next 28 years. The BCR still carried through freight and special passenger trains until West Riding freight rationalisation in the early 1960s returned it to a branch serving just Wharncliffe Woodmoor Colliery. That remaining section from Stairfoot was abandoned in May, 1967.

The LNER then axed its Cudworth-Hull passenger trains on 1st January, 1932. The

This St. Pancras to Bradford express was one of several express passenger and goods trains which took the Chapeltown Loop via Monk Spring Junction and Cudworth. With grubby Jubilee 4-6-0 No. 45562 *Alberta* in charge it is seen storming towards Monk Spring during June, 1958. *(Peter Sunderland)*

H&B also continued as a through freight line, until 6th April, 1959, when it closed east of Wrangbrook Junction, the point where branches to Wath and Denaby left the main line. Remaining traffic was routed towards Cudworth until 7th August, 1967 when the line closed between there and Wrangbrook.

The rest of the 1930s and 40s saw only minor cutbacks - but then came the 1950s and a devastating assault on the passenger network.

Practically everything except trains on the Midland main line and today's Sheffield-Barnsley-Leeds route was wiped out.

The Dearne Valley service was withdrawn in September, 1951 leaving the line freight only for its remaining 15 years. GC line Barnsley-Sheffield trains ran for the last time on 5th December, 1953. The Court House-Cudworth shuttle was axed on 9th June, 1958, replaced by Leeds-Barnsley Exchange diesels which were so popular that they brought a 263 per cent increase in passengers during the first year. The Penistone-Doncaster service stopped running from 29th June, 1959, although the Penistone and Mexborough lines continued to be used by summer Saturday trains and a through overnight carriage from Manchester which was attached to a newspaper train until the Woodhead line passenger service was withdrawn in January, 1970. The news vans ran via Barnsley until 1973.

Goods lines closed in the 1950s included the Wharncliffe branch in stages between 1954 and 1959, its industrial customers just as easily served by the parallel GC line. The Old Oaks Junction to Oakwell line, the Cudworth-Barnsley line between Monk Bretton and Barnsley West(including spectacular Oaks Viaduct), the goods facilities at Oakwell and Old Mill Lane, the Cudworth South to West curve, and Wentworth station all went in 1959.

That same year, engineers revealed that the girder bridge carrying the eastern approach to Barnsley Court House station needed repairs costing £200,000.

Only Sheffield Midland locals used Court House by then and BR found that concentrating all remaining passenger services on Exchange station would cost only half as much and allow through running between Sheffield and Leeds.

New connections at Quarry Junction gave Sheffield Midland trains access to Exchange via the Mexborough line which had to be raised by up to 14ft to meet it. The Quarry Junction-Court House line was abandoned and the worn out girder bridge scrapped. Exchange station was upgraded and a second platform added for Sheffield-bound trains.

Everything came to a head over Easter, 1960 and all the changes, including introduction of the Sheffield-Leeds diesel service running today, took effect on 19th April following a three-day shutdown to complete the work. Court House, still connected to the Penistone line, was used for goods and parcels until being abandoned on 31st January, 1966.

There was little passenger railway left around Barnsley for Beeching to axe in the 1960s, but the drive to reduce duplication of colliery connections saw several goods lines closed completely.

The Stairfoot-Houghton branch shut in October, 1960 and the Monk Spring-Cudworth line in September, 1964, cutting off the Chapeltown Loop. From 11th july, 1966 the Grimethorpe-Goldthorpe section of the Dearne Valley was connected to the Midland main line by a new Dearne Valley Junction, south of Cudworth, making the Grimethorpe-Crofton portion redundant.

Also that year, the GC Chapeltown line was gutted to save the cost of a new motorway bridge, leaving just branches from Wombwell to Rockingham and Smithywood to Tinsley.

In 1967, the H&B Cudworth Yard-Stairfoot and Midland Cudworth Station-Monk Spring lines were combined to form a new Cudworth Stairfoot line. Opened on 3rd July it avoided Ardsley Tunnel and gave direct access from the Midland main line to Wath yard.

Even the Midland main line was not immune. Its fortunes began to fall, rise and fall again like the mining subsidence that so blighted the railways of the area.

Stopping passenger trains were withdrawn and Royston and Cudworth stations closed on 1st January, 1968. The Royston Junction-Thornhill line followed in May and from 7th October the expresses were rerouted via Moorthorpe and the Swinton & Knottingley line to avoid crippling speed restrictions caused by mining subsidence.

The Midland remained busy with freight as did Cudworth and Carlton yards but the writing was on the wall. They escaped closure following completion of the big Healey Mills marshalling yard in 1963 but traffic was declining. The shrinking yards were doomed to end up used for storing wagons. Steam had ended too and Royston shed was reduced to a diesel signing-on point before closing altogether in September, 1971 along with Carlton North and H&B yards.

Events of 1968 were reversed five years later when even worse subsidence turned the S&K into a low-speed roller coaster while that under the main line was ending. BR upgraded the line through Cudworth for Cross-Country InterCity trains, even those from the North East which had always used the S&K.

With introduction of High Speed Trains in 1981, resignalling and 115mph running were proposed under a £10.4 million upgrade for the whole North East-South West route, but the plan was short-lived.

New BR InterCity management, grappling with recession, coach competition and a serious earth slip at Chevet, rerouted their trains back to the S&K or via Doncaster in 1983, leaving only freight and two summer dated trains, the Friday 22.39 Bradford - Paignton and 07.39 Leicester-Scarborough until they too were diverted after summer, 1986.

What then remained of the Barnsley rail network became a victim of the systematic destruction of Britain's coal industry.

In 1979, the National Coal Board began combining underground systems so that coal could be brought to the surface at just three big modernised pits - Woolley(Darton), Houghton Main and South Kirkby. Bulk loading bunkers would feed merry-go-round trains leaving every half hour for the big power stations. Local rail-served pits like Dodworth, North Gawber, Barrow and Royston drift would close by the mid-1980s.

But no sooner were the bunkers commissioned than they were made redundant by the Government's pit closure programme which wiped out the whole Barnsley coalfield and rail-born coal traffic with it.

The Midland main line was totally abandoned between Houghton Main and Wath Road Junction by 1988. Since then the colliery and Coalite works at Grimethorpe have gone along with what remained of the Dearne Valley. By spring, 1996 the Midland

During four months in 1960, the whole shape of Barnsley's railway changed dramatically with all remaining passenger trains concentrated on Exchange station and Court House reduced to a dead end parcels shed. The key to this was the remodelling at Quarry Junction, where a new layout enabled Sheffield Midland trains to reach Exchange station. This Derby Heavyweight diesel unit crossing the bridge over the Mexborough line with the 6.30pm to Sheffield, was the last train to use Court House and the old route on Good Friday 15th April, 1960. *(David Green)*

The reopening of the Barnsley-Penistone line to regular passenger services and a new station at Silkstone Common was the most significant move towards a rail revival around Barnsley in the 1980s. This was the original Silkstone station in the 1950s with ex-Great Central J11 0-6-0 No. 64417 on a Court House-Penistone stopper. *(Neville Stead collection)*

main line consisted of a goods branch carrying one sand train running a couple of days a week to the Redfearn glass works at Monk Bretton. That is now the only freight in the whole Barnsley area.

The remaining chunks of the GC Chapeltown line were eradicated in the mid-1980s upon closure of Barrow Colliery and Smithywood coking plant. Wath yard, very much reduced since closure of the Woodhead line in 1981, and all the railway from Quarry Junction to Mexborough and Stairfoot to Cudworth went around the same time.

At least it was not all doom and gloom.

In 1977, the South Yorkshire Passenger Transport Executive began subsidising the Barnsley-Sheffield service, securing its future. The PTE's political masters favoured buses at first but they eventually recognised the value of a useful rail system and a modest revival began.

The Penistone line reopened to passengers as the happy outcome of a complex funding battle and political brinkmanship in which the Huddersfield-Sheffield service faced three closure proposals in a year.

During a public hearing into the second proposal, South Yorkshire PTE dramatically announced that it would support an experimental service diverted through Barnsley instead of using the remaining Penistone-Sheffield portion of the Woodhead line.

In 75 days, BR singled the line between Dodworth and Penistone, and upgraded track and signalling so that passenger trains could run via Barnsley from 16th May, 1983. New stations have since opened at Silkstone (Silkstone Common) and Dodworth and the service is going from strength to strength.

By 1996, Barnsley was probably served by more trains than ever with three each way an hour, composed of Sheffield-Leeds, Wakefield and Huddersfield services. Between 1986 and 1989 it even had an InterCity 125 to and from St. Pancras.

By May, 1992, Exchange station had been rebuilt as an £8 million bus/rail interchange boasting the latest passenger facilities.

In 1991, a PTE strategy document said that Barnsley line signalling should be modernised and suggested new stations at Haigh, Stairfoot and Skiers Spring. Five years later none of the proposals had materialised while the yawning gap between Barnsley and Mexborough inhibits travel between the town, Doncaster, and the East Coast main line.

There seems to be little hope of a freight revival and one can only wonder how much longer Cudworth and Royston will remain on the railway map.

CUDWORTH & ROYSTON

Above: Viewed from Middlestown Junction signal box on the Royston Junction-Thornhill line on 28th June, 1958, Black Five 4-6-0 No.45279 comes up from Thornhill Junction with a summer Saturday Blackpool-Sheffield express. The original main line to Dewsbury(centre) went no further than the bridge over the L&Y main line by this time and was used for wagon storage. On the left is the westbound line down to Thornhill Junction.

Below: On the same day, 8F 2-8-0 No. 48169 was coming the other way with a Carlton to Mytholmroyd coal train. *(Both Tony Ross)*

The nine-mile Royston Jn.-Thornhill Midland Jn. line provided a useful link between the Midland and Lancashire and Yorkshire main lines, and gave direct access to the Midland's own goods depots at Dewsbury and Huddersfield.

It was an undulating road with a series of rising and falling 1 in 200 gradients culminating in a one-mile 1 in 120 descent to Thornhill Junction where it joined the L&Y Wakefield-Manchester line.

Its main feature was the imposing Crigglestone viaduct which, although trackless, still spans the Wakefield-Barnsley line.

There were stations and signal boxes at Crigglestone(named Crigglestone East from 1924 to avoid confusion with the L&Y station) and Middlestown. Crigglestone was three miles 1232 yards from Royston Junction and Middlestown seven miles 362 yards.

The goods depot at Middlestown closed in 1937 but Crigglestone East stayed in business until February, 1964.

Signalling was absolute block but permissive block was allowed on the Up line between Crigglestone East and Royston Junction for trains not carrying passengers. Absolute block was in force if Crigglestone East box was closed. Track circuit block was used between Thornhill and Middlestown Junction from 1963 when Thornhill Midland Jn. box closed.

Apart from a Bradford-Sheffield express started by the L&Y and the Bradford Exchange -St Pancras 'Yorkshireman', both of which stopped running by the 1940s, the only passenger trains were summer Saturday excursions.

The line was well used by freight and mineral trains, though, until it finally closed in 1968. Most were class J coal trains going west and class F empties returning.

The Royston to Thornhill line was to have had stations at Middlestown and Crigglestone East but there were never any stopping trains to use them. These were the bare platforms at Middlestown, looking east, in 1963. *(Roger Hepworth)*

Royston-Thornhill line booked freight 2.11.59 - 2.6.60

Time	Days	Train	Time	Days	Train
1.55am	MX	Carlton North-Mirfield	2.50am	MThO	Mirfield-Matlock empties*(suspended)*
3.20am		Royston Jn. - Middlestown Jn.	2.10am	MX	Rose Grove-Cudworth empties
3.50am	MX	Carlton North-Mytholmroyd	3.55am	MX	Middlestown Jn-Manvers Main empties
6.35am	MO	Carlton North-Mirfield	8.10am	MO	Mirfield-Carlton North LE & brakevan
6.35am	MX	Carlton North-Moston	8.30am		Bradley Wood-Manvers Main
7.40am	MX	Manvers Main-Sowerby Bridge LE	8.8am	MSX	Rose Grove-Carlton North empties
9am	MX	Carlton North-Mytholmroyd	7.2am	SX	Bamber Bridge-Manvers Main empties
9.20am		Carlton South-Crigglestone class K	12.15pm		Crigglestone East-Carlton North class K
4.18am	SX	Toton-Middlestown class F	1.45pm	SX	Mirfield-Crigglestone East
7.28am	WFO	Barrow-Crigglestone East empties	1.7pm		Middleton Jn-Manvers Main empties
2.25pm		Carlton North-Rose Grove	1.30pm	SX	Aintree-Seymour Jn empties
3.25pm	S X	Crigglestone East--Mytholmroyd	4.10pm	SO	Rose Grove-Cudworth empties
4pm		Carlton North - Mytholmroyd	7.20pm	SX	Cleckheaton-Carlton South class D
1pm	TFO	Matlock-Mirfield class F*(suspended)*	9.35pm	SX	Bradley Wood-Manvers Main empties
9pm	SX	Carlton North-Rose Grove	7pm	SX	Bamber Bridge-Manvers Main empties
9pm	SO	Carlton North-Mirfield*(suspended)*			

LE: light engine

Above: **Royston-based WD 2-8-0 No. 90243 stands at Crigglestone East home signal in January, 1962 with a westbound loaded coal train. It was held up waiting for ice to be cleared from Crigglestone tunnel, a short distance ahead.** *(D.N.Carter)*

SHORT MEMORIES

21.9.57: New 350hp diesel shunters D3375-80 allocated to Royston.

1.10.58: The Condor express container train makes its first run. Metrovick Co-Bos D5700 & D5701 pass through Cudworth hauling 24 Lowfit wagons of 18 tons each. Every one and the brake van has roller bearings with the aim of travelling from Hendon to Glasgow in 6 hours.

2.10.58: Royston 1P 0-4-4T No. 58066 is withdrawn after a long period in store.

WORKING OVER THE UP LINE BETWEEN CRIGGLESTONE EAST STATION AND ROYSTON JN. SIGNAL BOXES. The first train or locomotive running light requiring to pass over the Up line after Permissible Block working has been in operation will be brought under control at the Home signal for Crigglestone East station box. After the signal has been taken off for the train to proceed the signalman will exhibit a green hand signal which the driver must acknowledge by a short whistle, and must understand that he must proceed with caution throughout the section to Royston Junction. *(Eastern Region(North Area) Sectional Appendix, 1968.*

Below: The layout at Crigglestone East in 1960 showing the interesting arrangement of colliery connections. The photographer of the above picture would be standing with his back to the goods yard, about opposite the signal box. *(Not to scale)*

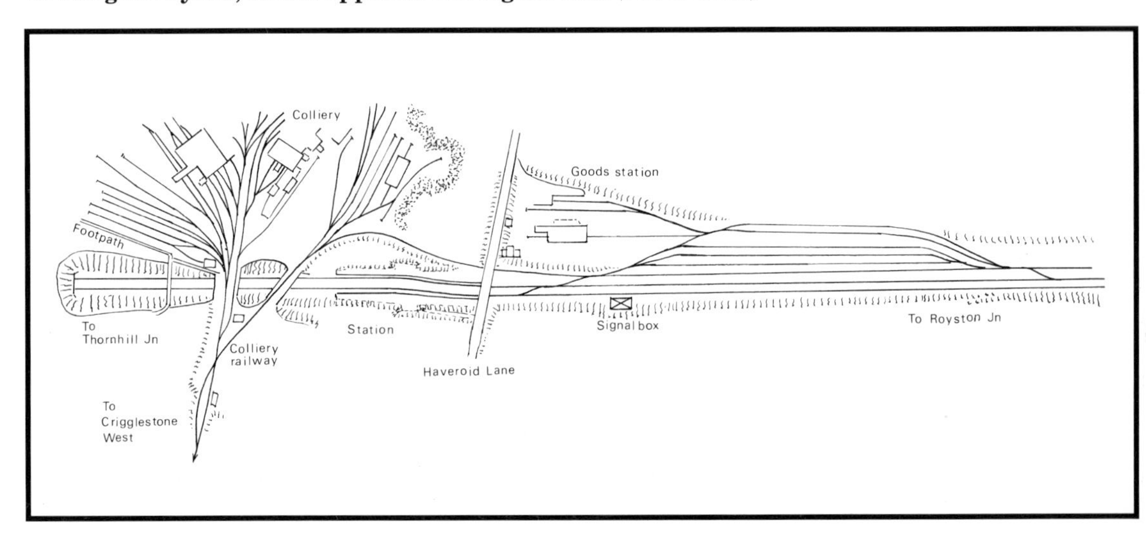

Above: This delightful scene on a beautiful summer's day in the early 1950s shows Kettering-based LMS-built Compound 4-4-0 No. 41063 heading a southbound semi-fast over Royston Junction. The Thornhill line diverged to the left but in March, 1996 only a double track remained and even then only one line was in use. *(Peter Ackley)*

Below: 4F 0-6-0 No. 44099 was on the 7.26am Cudworth to Leeds all stations when Holbeck fireman Roy Wood caught it overtaking his goods train between Royston and Royston Junction on 7th June, 1962.

In 1960 the Midland main line through Cudworth and Royston had signal boxes at Storrs Mill Junction(1 mile 484 yards south of Cudworth Station box), Cudworth South Junction(770 yards north of Cudworth Station), Cudworth North Junction(814 yds), Carlton Main Sidings(946 yds), Carlton North Sidings(470 yds - controlled goods lines only), Royston & Notton(784 yds), Hodroyd's & Monckton Main Sidings(1342yds), Royston Junction(704 yds). Cudworth Station North was by then abolished and Cudworth Station South renamed Cudworth Station.

Signalling was absolute block on the Main or Fast lines and on the Slow lines(between Cudworth station and Royston Junction), and permissive block on the Goods lines south of Cudworth station. An additional Up Goods line between Royston & Notton and Carlton North Sidings was permissive block and had no block between Carlton North and Main. By 1968, signalling on the Main/Fast and Slow lines was track circuit block. Maximum speed on Main/Fast lines was 70mph with 40mph on the Goods lines.

Above: A scene of veritable tranquility in an industrial landscape compared to the noise and fumes of today's road-mad society. Rotherham Canklow-based 8F 2-8-0 No. 48026 rolls a heavy load of goods along the Up Fast through Royston station on 5th September, 1962. The Monckton Coke and Chemical company's plant dominated the skyline then as it does in 1996. *(Peter Rose)*

Below: An unusual view from the cab of a northbound diesel of Jubilee 4-6-0 No. 45675 *Hardy* while it was calling at Royston with an Up stopping train on 10th April, 1964. (*Roy Wood)*

Left: Tom Newsome(3rd left) was Peter Rose's father-in-law and worked on the LMS at Royston for a while before joining the army. Like many rail staff then, he was sent away from home (Leeds) to work. He found lodgings at The Ship Hotel where he made extra money by acting as odd job man.
The gas lamp has Midland Railway etched in the glass and the poster advertises an excursion to Cadbury's chocolate factory at Bournville.
(Peter Rose collection)
This station dated from 1900, having replaced the North Midland Railway original a mile further north.

Right: Royston station, or Royston and Notton to give it its full title, shut on 1st January, 1968 when local services were withdrawn, but the station building was still intact, if empty, on 25th May, 1970.
(M.A.King / Barnsley Library))
Some alterations had been made since the above picture was taken. The chimneys had been rebuilt and the parcels office (nearest the camera in the above picture) demolished, but the original platform direction signs were still in place on the extreme left.

ROYSTON & NOTTON DEPARTURES, SUMMER 1957

7.28am 6.39am Leeds City-Sheffield
9.12am 8.20am Leeds City-Sheffield
1.23pm SO 12.39pm Leeds City-Cudworth
2.4pm 1.15pm Leeds City-Sheffield
4.22pmSO 1.50pm Morecambe-Nottingham
(20th July-7th September)
4.33pmSX 4.15pm from Normanton
(School days only)
4.42pmSO 2.20pm Blackpool N-Sheffield
4.59pm 4.11pm Leeds City-Sheffield
6.10pm SX 5.25pm Leeds City-Cudworth
6.32pm 5.25pm Bradford FS-Sheffield
7.4pm 6.21pm Leeds City-Cudworth
7.48pm 6.5pm Bradford FS-Derby
9.2pm 8.20pm Leeds City-Sheffield
9.33pm 8.51pm Leeds City-Sheffield
10.56pmSO 8.50pm Bradford FS-St Pancras
10.56pmSX 9.20pm Bradford FS-St Pancras

6.23am 6.18am Cudworth-Leeds City
7.25am 7.20am Cudworth-Leeds City
7.52am SO 6.50am Sheffield-Blackpool N.
(12th July-7th September)
8.6am SX 7.12am Sheffield-Leeds City
8.13am SO 7.12am Sheffield-Leeds City
9am SO 5.50am Nottingham-Morecambe
(13th July-31st August)
10.53am 7.55am Nottingham-Bradford FS
12.16pmSO 11.25am Sheffield-Leeds City
12.30pmSX 11.40am Sheffield-Leeds City
2.11pm SO 2.6pm Cudworth-Leeds City
3.16pm 12.20pm Nottingham-Leeds City
5.5pm 4.15pm Sheffield-Leeds City
8.18pm 7.25pm Sheffield-Leeds City
11pm 10.15pm Sheffield-Leeds City

On 10th September, 1964 a goods train came to grief at Royston station with resulting devastation of track and wagons, some ending up on the platforms.
Above: Looking north towards the station with breakdown cranes clearing up the mess - and what seems to be plenty of experts offering advice. The roof of the goods shed is just visible between the cranes. *(Roy Wood)*

Below: Local 4F No. 44582 on trip working 48 ventures into the deep grass of closed Royston goods yard on 1st September, 1962. The goods office is behind the engine. *(Peter Rose)*

SHORT MEMORIES

25.12.58: Britannia 4-6-2 No.70054 *Dornoch Firth* heads the Down Thames-Clyde Express via Chapeltown.

24.7.59: Britannia No. 70042 *Lord Roberts* of Manchester Trafford Park is on the 11.36 Sheffield-Leeds local and 4.11pm return.

21.6.60: Class 2 2-6-0 No. 46494 of Sheffield Millhouses works the 8.44am Halifax-St Pancras, and again on 22.7.60.

27.6.60: BR Standard No. 78024 is on the morning and evening Halifax trains.

Above: Crewe North Black Five No. 45225 was unusual power for the 4.15pm Leeds City to Sheffield stopper, seen pausing at an intact Royston station on 29th May, 1962. The train was booked for a Leeds Holbeck engine. *(Peter Rose)*

Below: 4F 0-6-0 No. 44446 brings the 7.26am Cudworth to Leeds into Royston station on 5th June, 1962. On the right is East End Crescent, the housing estate built by the LMS in the early 1930s for its staff at the newly opened Royston engine shed. *(Peter Rose)*

LIFE AT ROYSTON

Tom Hicks was a Royston locoman from 1934 until the end of steam when he transferred to Healey Mills.

"My family moved from near Nuneaton in the early 1930s to a new house on the railway estate.

"The houses were grouped round an ash square, where a small hand pump fire engine was kept ready for use by a small brigade of four or five men in case there was a house fire. But I don't think it was ever needed.

"The shed had 10 roads with water columns and pits, each capable of holding two 8Fs and a small loco.

"Overhead cranes were installed along with a wheel drop pit which was soon taken out again because engines were supposed to go to Holbeck for major repairs.

"The one line leading to the depot had a water column alongside, so anyone stopping there for water blocked the whole shed in.

"There was a unique coaling machine which picked the whole wagon up and not only tipped its contents into a hopper, but also the oil from its axleboxes. The coal fell into a pit directly underneath. From there a conveyor carried it in buckets up a 30ft tower under which engines stood to receive the coal. After coaling, engines went to the ashpit.

"There was no turntable, just a triangle. When the Hull and Barnsley shed closed a connection was installed from the triangle to the H&B line to get engines out that way.

"We had a lot of trouble with the water which was always causing engines to prime. They tried putting balls of chemicals in the tank but if a train was going to Leeds or Rotherham, we left the tender feed open, ran the water away through the overflow and refilled with good water when we got there.

"I was 15 when I started at Royston, working 11pm to 7am calling up. There were two of us - one did the Crescent, over 200 houses, and the other did houses over a wider area."

When the second world war began, Tom joined the army and was one of the first men parachuted into Arnhem.

In the army he passed for driving at the Longmoor Military Railway and on de-mob was able to go back to Royston as a fireman, passing the driver's exams in four months.

"After the war, a lot of Royston's men were quite young and the Lanky men who relieved us at Sowerby Bridge or Mytholmroyd called us Royston's baby drivers.

"We booked on at 12.40am for the Garston turn, taking coal to the banana boats. Pre-war, Royston sent Derby 'Austin 7' 0-8-0s, Crab 2-6-0s, a pair of L&Y class 'A' 0-6-0s, 4Fs or L&Y 0-8-0s. Sometimes we had a Wessy 'Super D' 0-8-0 - terrible engines. The 8Fs came about 1938 going onto the Garston.

"We lodged there and worked coal empties, cattle or a Llandudno-Leeds excursion back.

"We took the 'Barrow Babies' - a train of yellow coke wagons - to Carnforth. They had names on the sides saying the type of steel the coke would be used for. A polished 8F with this train looked very nice.

"We worked Garratts to and from Toton with coal or coke for Thorncliffe steelworks, and took iron ore from Wellingborough to Normanton where we handed over to North Eastern engines and men.

"We called the Crigglestone East line the Golden Mile because we could get held up there for eight hours or more.

"Carlton yard had 30-40 roads but the South yard had only two receptions so five or six trains could be backed up the main line. At West Riding box, beyond Walton station, they would bring us to a stand and hold up a green light to say there was a train in front. Some signalmen held their fingers up to say how many trains there were. Some didn't and on a dark night you would hang out the side looking for the tail light of the train in front.

"We brought empties for Carlton Colliery on the Down side. To reach the spur to the colliery sidings we had to cross all four main lines with 25 or 30 wagons and from 9pm to midnight we couldn't move - it was so busy.

"We had local passenger turns and express work if, say, the Down Devonian was late and we relieved the Birmingham men at Cudworth so they could get home again.

"When the H&B shed closed we began working to Hull. It was a nice run, countryside all the way. At one level crossing during the night an old lady used to come out in her night gown to open the gates for us before going back to bed."

Above: Having called at Royston station on 28th May, 1962, Jubilee No. 45694 *Bellerophon* gets in to its stride past the motive power depot with the 4.15pm Leeds City-Sheffield Midland. On the right, class 4F and 8F engines await their turn at the coaler. *(Peter Rose)*

Below: Royston shed yard from the main line embankment on 27th August, 1962. On view are 8F 2-8-0 No. 48466, WD 2-8-0 No. 90591, 'Crab' 2-6-0 No. 42762 and Midland 4F No. 43914 - a good cross-section of Royston 1960s power.. Typical of big steam sheds are the ash hopper, wooden wagons loaded with ashes, drums of oil put to the ground, a coal stack and the raised water tank. *(Peter Rose)*

Royston motive power depot was built from scratch by the LMS in the early 1930s. Its main job was to provide engines for the extensive mineral workings emanating from Carlton yards but it also kept a few passenger engines for local services like the Cudworth-Barnsley push-pull and stopping trains to Leeds.
Royston's role was expanded in 1951 when it took over the workings of the Hull and Barnsley shed at Cudworth.
Coded 20C in the BR London Midland Region Leeds Holbeck district, Royston became 55D when the whole district was transferred to the North Eastern Region in 1957. It was the last shed in the West Riding to use steam, its last steam working being a goods to Goole on 4th November, 1967. The shed remained in use for diesels and retained a small allocation of diesel shunters until finally closing altogether in September, 1971 when the shunters were dispersed to Healey Mills and Bradford Hammerton Street.
When Peter Rose took the fine picture above on 27th August, 1962 we would not have spared such a line up of black goods engines a second look, preferring instead to wait for green namers on the main line behind us. What we would give for a sight like this today. From left are 8F 2-8-0 48473, 'Crab' 2-6-0 42762, 8Fs 48670 and 48337, and WD 2-8-0s 90488 and 90132.

LOCOMOTIVES ALLOCATED TO ROYSTON

Summer, 1950. Stanier class 3 2-6-2T: 40074/147/81/93; Johnson 2P 4-4-0: 40444/521; Fairburn 4MT 2-6-4T: 42142/3/5; Johnson 3F 0-6-0: 43233/50/332/446/553/765/89; MR 4F 0-6-0: 43942/4003; LMS 4F 0-6-0: 44141/61/446; 3F 0-6-0T: 47421/48/62/581/634; 8F 2-8-0: 48062/78/ 80/93/5/103/ 13/ 62/9/337/76/7/412/9/31/9/43/532/40/2; Aspinall 3F 0-6-0: 52095/108/252/8; Hughes 3F 0-6-0: 52559; Johnson 1P 0-4-4T: 58052/66/75/90; Johnson 2F 0-6-0: 58156/88/237/60/5. Total: 60.

July, 1962: Drewry 0-6-0 diesel: D2266; 350hp 0-6-0 diesel: D3376/7/8/9/458/937/41; Stanier 3MT 2-6-2T: 40148/93; `Crab' 5P5F 2-6-0: 42762/70/95; MR 4F 0-6-0: 43906/14/42/83; LMS 4F 0-6-0: 44098/9/274/90/446/582; 8F 2-8-0: 48067/70/8/93/113/23/30/46/59/62/9/222/81/337/439/43/66/73/ 532/7/ 40/ 670/710; WD 2-8-0: 90127/243/336/95/407/88/511/91/605/10/1/50/84. Total: 59

On 20th May, 1967, Royston shed received Drewry class 04 0-6-0 diesel shunters Nos. D2271/2 from Holbeck. In 1996, D2272 was still going strong at a coal depot in Blackburn, Lancs.

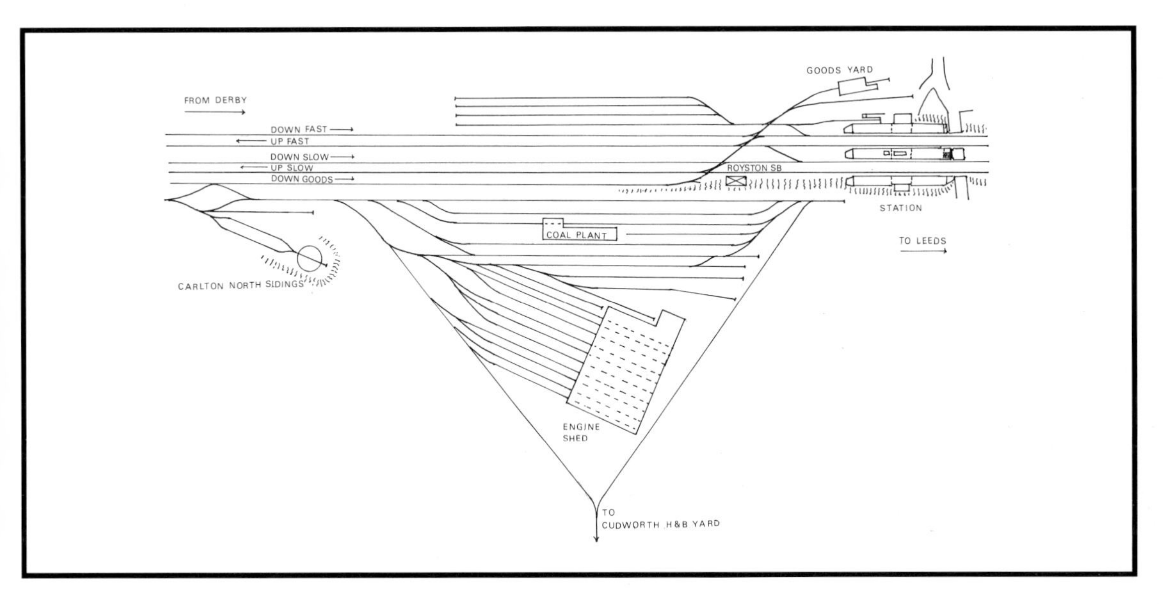

Above: Royston shed and station in the 1950s. *(Not to scale)*

LOCOMOTIVES ALLOCATED TO ROYSTON

November, 1966: 4MT 2-6-0: 43076/7/8/9; 8F 2-8-0: 48067/70/5/113/23/46/59/60/2/9/222/81/337/52/94/439/66/73/537/40/710/21; WD 2-8-0: 90318/605/15/42/5/50; Drewry 0-6-0 diesel: D2266; 350hp 0-6-0 diesel: D3377/8/9/458/937/41. Total: 39

Below: WD 2-8-0 No. 90127 and BR Standard class 5 4-6-0 No. 73161, both types which were later additions to the Royston fleet, stand in the sun outside the shed on 5th September, 1962. *(Peter Rose)*

Three ages of Midland 0-6-0 at Royston.
Top: Johnson 2F No. 58260, a type dating from 1878 but rebuilt around 1917 with 5ft 3in driving wheels, smaller boiler and Belpaire firebox, on 1st December, 1956.

Below: The 3Fs dated from 1885 but were rebuilt from 1916 by Fowler with Belpaire fireboxes. No. 43714 was nearby, among the ash and coal plants. *(Both David Holmes)*

Right: One of Fowler's own 4Fs for the LMS, No. 44290, in Royston shed on 5th September, 1962. *(Peter Rose)*

Johnson's Midland 1P 0-4-4Ts were once regular power for the Cudworth-Barnsley push-pull. No. 58066 was one of Royston's fleet for this job but its working life was over when stored next to Royston & Notton signal box on 13th July, 1958. *(Graham Kaye)*

ROYSTON MOTIVE POWER DEPOT LINE TO CUDWORTH YARD NORTH: An illuminated Stop Board with telephone is fixed at the exit from the depot, 60 yards from the points of the triangle, on the line leading to Cudworth Yard North signal box ... No locomotive must pass this board until permission has been obtained verbally from the Cudworth Yard North signalman...Locomotives entering the depot must travel via the left hand route on the triangle, whether turning or coming from the direction of Cudworth Yard North....
Traffic from Cudworth Yard H&B for Royston depot may be worked via Cudworth Yard North and the depot line during daylight and clear weather only under the same conditions as light engines. Trains must not exceed 10 wagons and a brake van.... *North Eastern Region Sectional Appendix, 1960.*

Below: Hull Dairycoates WD No. 90688 clanks round the Royston shed triangle before taking a return load from Carlton sidings in June, 1962. By this time it could have not reached Royston by the Hull and Barnsley and its route would be via Goole. *(Peter Rose)*

Above: Royston shed looked bare on 27th March, 1971 but there were still plenty of diesels inside, class 37s and 40s having succeeded the 8Fs and WDs. The end was nigh, however, and six months later the shed was closed altogether. *(Adrian Booth)*

LOCOMOTIVES ON ROYSTON SHED

22nd August, 1970

Class 40: 396; Class 37: 6735/6914/18/25/9/50; Class 08 0-6-0: 3378/458/876/937; Class 11 0-6-0: 12113.

Below: Well polished Black Five 4-6-0 No. 44962 from Saltley shed, Birmingham, was following the 7.26am Cudworth to Leeds local passenger when passing the distinctive Carlton North Sidings signal box with an express freight on 5th June, 1962. The start of Carlton North yard is on the left while the wagons in the distant right are on the Wharncliffe Woodmoor colliery railway leading up to Carlton Main colliery. The train is just passing over the H&B Wharncliffe Woodmoor branch. *(Peter Rose)*

No locomotive must proceed in the direction of Carlton North Sidings signal box on the locomotive line, although the signal may be in the "clear" position, until permission has been obtained from the signalman, who must be informed which direction the locomotive requires to run to Carlton North Sidings. *N.E. Region Sectional Appendix, 1960.*

Above: The timber construction of lofty Carlton North Sidings signal box dated only from the 1950s.. It is shown to good effect in this northwards looking view of 4F No. 44584 on 27th August, 1962. In the background, a WD 2-8-0 is standing on the turntable line. *(Peter Rose)*

Below: The extent of Carlton yards can be appreciated from this panormaic view of Wakefield 'Crab' No. 42861 heading along the Up Slow past Carlton South sidings, also on 27th August, 1962.
(Peter Rose)

Down express freight trains passing Cudworth, Mondays to Fridays - Summer, 1960

12.5am	9.20pm		Nottingham - Carlisle London Road class C
12.30am	8pm	TWFO	Harpenden - Greenhill class C
1.8am	9.55pm	SX	Birmingham Lawley St. - Hunslet Down Sidings class C
1.12am	4.48pm		Bristol - Hunslet Lane class C
1.25am	9.50pm	FO	Birmingham Lawley St. - Hunslet Down Sidings class C
2.17am	10.40pm		Leicester - Hunslet Down Sidings class C
2.44am	10.52pm		Nottingham - Hunslet Down Sidings class D
3.34am	8.40pm		Somers Town - Hunslet Down Sidings class C
4.30am	12.20am	MX	Heaton Mersey - Hunslet Down Sidings class E
4.40am	9.45pm		Birmingham Lawley Street - Normanton North Yard class E
6.6am	12.30am	MX	St. Pancras - Hunslet Down Sidings class C
6.40am	2.30am	MO	Water Orton - Hunslet Down Sidings class E
6.51am	3.30am	MX	Water Orton - Hunslet Down Sidings class D
6.55am	3.50am		Water Orton - Carlisle class D
7.9am	3.57am	MX	Chaddesden - Hunslet Down Sidings class E
8.18am	1.55am	MSX	Willesden - Carlisle class C
8.35am	4.55am	MO	Chaddesden - Hunslet Down Sidings class E
4.22pm	9.30am		West End Sidings - Hunslet Down Sidings class C
5.14pm	2.25pm		Water Orton - Normanton Yard class C
7.36pm	4.45pm	SX	Water Orton - Glasgow class C
8.13pm	4.55pm		Water Orton - Carlisle class C
8.42pm	4.25pm	SX	Leicester - Carlisle Kingmoor class C
9.18pm	5.10pm		Water Orton - Hunslet Down Sidings class C
11.30pm	7.23pm		Hendon - Gushetfaulds class C *The Condor*
11.45pm	8.23pm		Burton(Wetmore) - Carlisle class C

Cadbury's chocolate and Dunlop rubber products were prime cargoes for trains from the Birmingham area.

Below: The complex layout at Cudworth and Carlton in 1931 and little changed for the next 20 years. *Reproduced from a 1 in 2500 Ordnance Survey Map by courtesy of the Ordnance Survey.*

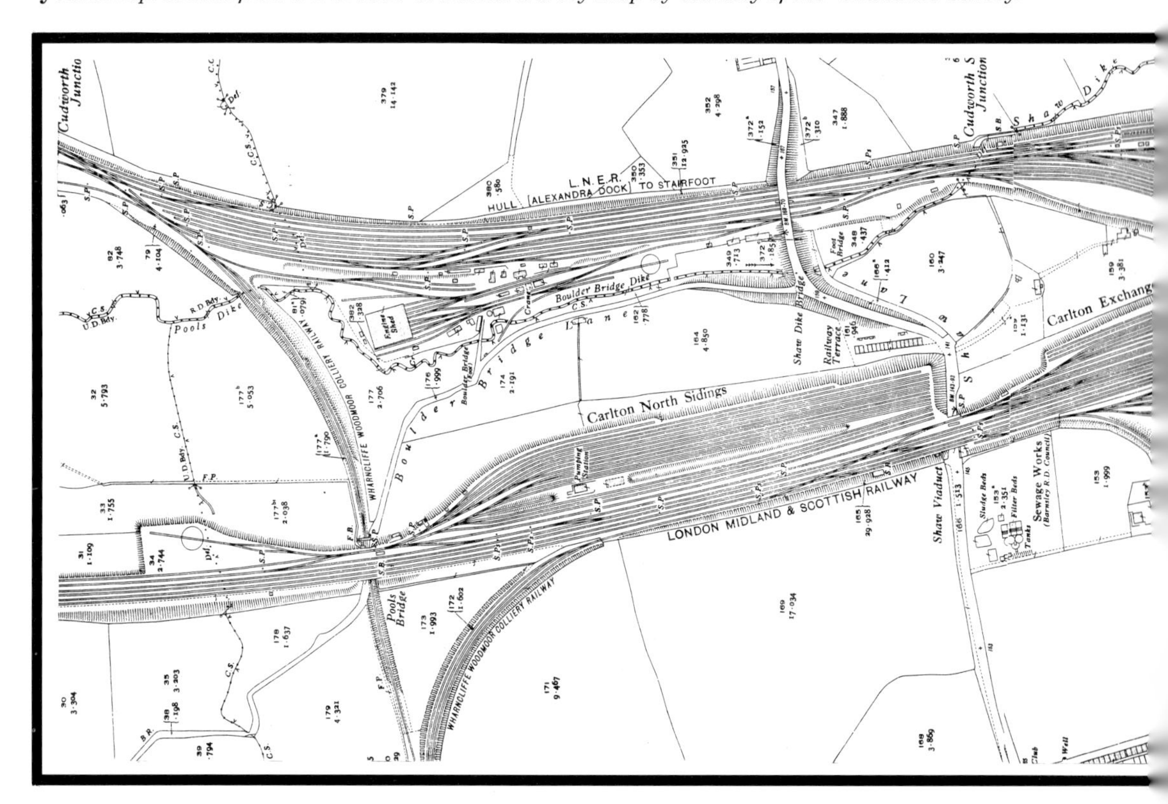

Above: In 1960, more than two dozen express freight trains passed Carlton yards in each direction every 24 hours as well as the 80 or more trip and mineral workings which came and went. This express freight was being eased along the Up Goods line at Carlton South by Wellingborough 9F 2-10-0 No. 92056 on 27th August, 1962. The headlamps show that 20 per cent of the train was fitted with automatic brake. *(Peter Rose)*

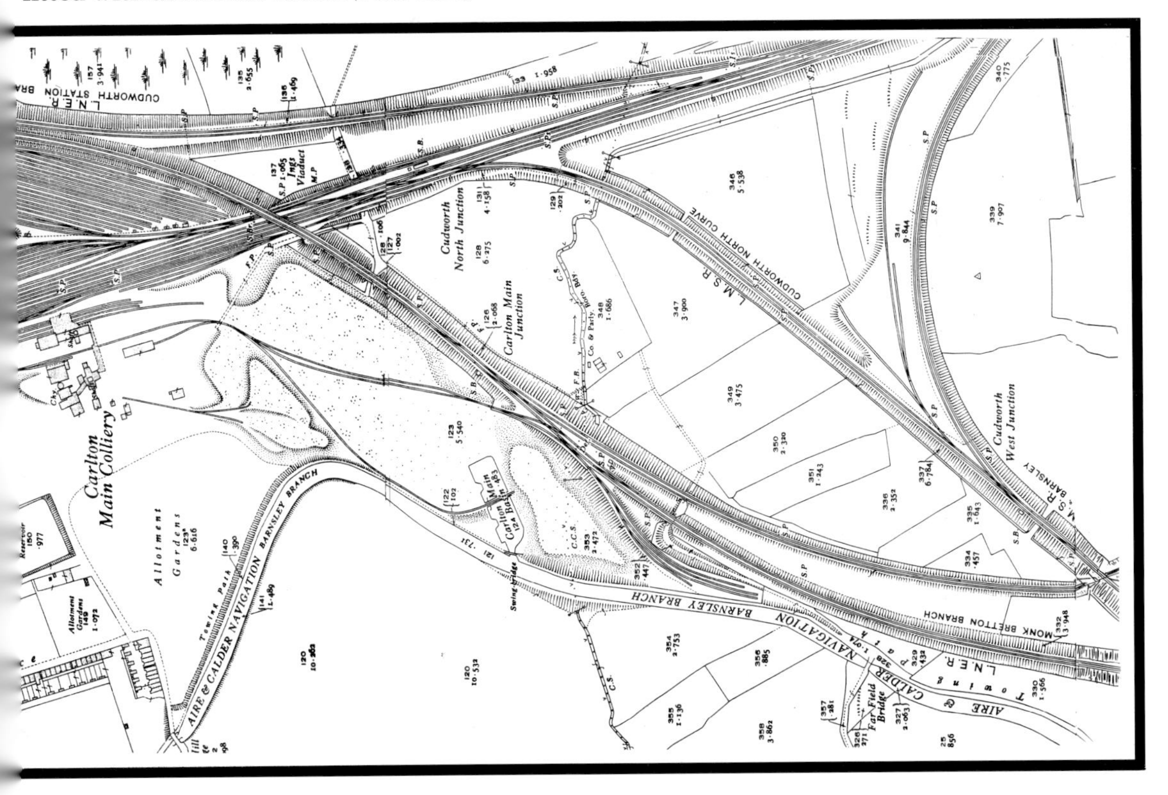

The time-honoured Barrow-Carlton empty coke wagons, alias the 'Barrow Babies' passes Wharncliffe Woodmoor No. 4 & 5 colliery(Carlton Main) on the left with Carlisle Black Five No. 45421 in charge during September, 1962. A few years earlier this was a job for a Royston 4F which took over from a Barrow 4F at Leeds Engine Shed Junction. This wonderful view was taken from the bridge carrying the Hull and Barnsley Stairfoot line. The H&B Cudworth South yard is on the right and the Midland Carlton South yard beyond the train. *(Peter Rose)*

Peter Rose made quite a few visits to Royston, both as a young enthusiast and in a professional capacity as a railwayman.

"My first visit to Royston shed was by bicycle on Sunday 4th September, 1949. Of the engines I saw, I recorded only my 'cops' which were 3F 0-6-0 43250, 4F 3942, 3F 0-6-0Ts 7421 and 7581, 8Fs 48076 of Westhouses, and 8540, 3F 0-6-0s 52095, 52108, 52252, 12558 and 52559, and 2F 0-6-0 58260.

"From Royston, I pedalled up to Barnsley where access to the shed was through a wicket gate at Jumble Lane level crossing. I recorded Q4 0-8-0s 63201, 3203, 63220, 3229, 63238, O4 2-8-0s 3687, 63802, 63840, 3904, J11 0-6-0s 64362, 4366, 64398, 64448, C13 4-4-2Ts 67409, 7411, 67434, N5 0-6-2Ts 9277, 9278, 9291, 69303, 69320, 9325, 9334, 69345, 9355,69357, 69365, 9367, and 69368, and O7 (WD) 2-8-0 77353(later 90253). This was my first visit so most engines were 'cops.' Of course, with the railways having only been nationalised for 21 months many engines still carried their old company numbers.

"I didn't know there was a shed at Cudworth too but went back there on 12th February, 1950, finding engines of North Eastern and Great Central origin - O7(WD) 2-8-0 63162, 04 2-8-0s 3667, 63732, 63849 and 63857, J25 0-6-0 65714 and A7 4-6-2T 69771. I found 30 engines on shed at Barnsley that day.

"During a train journey to Nottingham on 20th July, 1950 I noticed 'Super D' 0-8-0 49105 of Speke Junction on Royston shed. Shunting was still steam and 0-6-0Ts 47448 and 47462 were in Carlton yards. Ex-L&Y 0-6-0 52108 was at Cudworth - these engines were sent back to their native territory in

1952. On the way back I saw that 7581, still in LMS livery, had replaced 47448 in the yards while another L&Y 0-6-0, 52252, was present. Class 4 2-6-4Ts 42142 and 42145 were on shed with 4-4-0s 40444 and 40514.

"After passing out for firing duties at Holbeck at the end of 1950, I began to see Royston more often when firing on the main line. Going south from Normanton, after passing Walton station, we went through a deep cutting which old drivers said was a tunnel that had been opened out when the line was quadrupled. Beyond Royston Junction was a high bridge carrying the Barnsley-Nostell line but I don't recall ever seeing a train on it. Next, on the Up side, was Monckton colliery and coke works. On weekdays there was always plenty of activity with NCB and BR engines working.Once we were waiting orders in the signal box when a 3F 0-6-0 with two or three wagons moved up the line which curved round parallel to the Nostell line on the north side of the colliery yard before disappering from view. I did not know what was round the bend and the ensuing silence indicated the 3F had gone right away, but it did not have a brake van. While thinking about this I heard an engine working very hard and suddenly the 3F burst onto the scene, propelling its wagons at a ferocious speed and tearing through the colliery yard. I thought "has he gone mad?", but my driver and the signalman were unconcerned. Placing wagons in the company's sidings at the top of an incline on the south side of the colliery was an everyday occurrence and must have been the most spectacular work done by Royston men.

"In 1959 I left the footplate grade and, after training in the NE Region, was asked to take a look at working out of Cudworth H&B yard.

"After the H&B closed east of Barnsdale Tunnel in 1959, Hull pilots could no longer work through and all the collieries were then served from Cudworth yard during a single shift. I visited all the boxes and recorded much of the working with my pocket-sized Kodak Retinette 1B camera, helped by very good weather in the summer of 1962.

"At first, the line climbed northwards up a side valleybefore turning east. The Monckton waste tips were on the left and a new one was being started, the spoil tipped from a very high cableway. I once climbed the terminal mast here and from its moving and noisy summit took a shot of a 4F climbing from the yard. I did not stay for the next train!

"Facing points gave access to a reception line for trains of empty wagons bound for Monckton Main. Entry to the colliery branch was controlled by Monckton Empty Sidings box, built when a new east-facing connection to the branch replaced the previous one from Cudworth yard.

"The empties were worked from Cudworth yard onto the reception road, keeping the main line clear for following trains while they were reversed. On arrival at the box, the brake van was detached, the train drawing forward onto the dead end reversing siding before being propelled up the colliery branch over a low hill. The engines returned light, collected the van and went back to Cudworth yard, the loaded wagons going out on the Midland side."

The girder bridge carrying the Hull and Barnsley Stairfoot line over the Midland line was a Cudworth landmark. It was still in situ behind Cudworth North Junction signal box on 25th May, 1970, with Carlton Main colliery beyond. *(M. A. King/Barnsley Library.)*

Above: Grim conditions for a grim day - 8F No. 48222 wheezes past Cudworth South Junction box on 4th November, 1967, the last day of steam working from Royston shed. *(Adrian Booth)*

Below: BR Standard class 5 4-6-0 No. 73144, one of the batch fitted with Caprotti valve gear, draws its stopping train into Cudworth station during the 1950s. Coke wagons are stabled on the Hull & Barnsley line, right. *(Kenneth Field)*

SHORT MEMORIES

28.6.60: 4F 0-6-0 44188 of Walton, Liverpool, works the Halifax portion of the evening train from St. Pancras.

16.9.61: 8Fs 48067/159/443 are transferred to Royston. WDs 90127/407/684 follow a week later.

24.3.62: 4Fs 44098/99 are transferred from Normanton to Royston.

Sept, 1962: Brush Type 2 diesels take over Wath-Elland power station coal trains, Royston losing all its Elland workings.

Above: Cudworth station in the 1950s complete with water columns, Hull and Barnsley line on the right, and 4F No. 44290 rolling unfitted minerals along the Up Slow. *(Kenneth Field)*

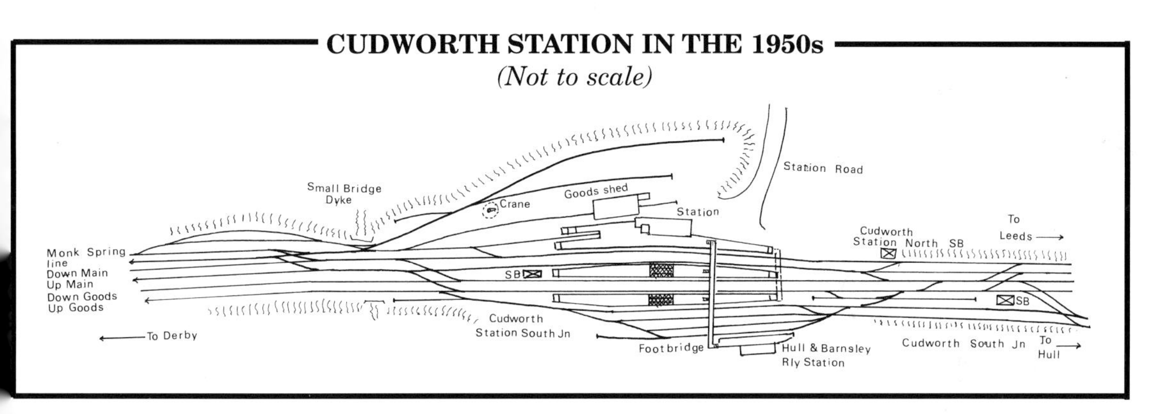

Right: Cudworth station closed to passengers on 1st January, 1968 and to goods on 4th May, 1964. It was starting to look a bit folorn when photographed from a Down train on 27th April, 1969. The footbridge was already being demolished, the portion to the H&B platform being all that was left. *(M.A.King / Barnsley Library)*

The summer, 1960 Working Timetable showed the 3.25am(MX) Bradford Forster Square-Derby empty coaching stock, due past Cudworth at 4.51am, as having the following load limits: Class 4P loco-370 tons, 4F loco-410 tons, Class 5 loco-425 tons, and Class 6P loco -480 tons.

PASSENGER TRAINS THROUGH CUDWORTH
Mondays-Fridays, Summer 1960

Down Direction

Time	Days	Dep.	Train
am			
12.11	MX	9.53pm	Nottingham-Bradford parcels
12.18	MO	9.43pm	Sutton Coldfield-Stirling car sleeper
12.41	ThO	9.35pm	" "
12.57	MWFO	7.45pm	Marylebone-Glasgow
1.35		9pm	St Pancras-Edinburgh
2.13		9.15pm	St Pancras-Glasgow
2.41		2.10am	Sheffield-Leeds mails
4.6	MX	3.35am	Sheffield-Leeds parcels
4.25	MX	9.40pm	St Pancras-Leeds parcels
4.53	MX	8.15pm	Bristol-Leeds parcels
5.12	MX	11.50pm	St Pancras-Leeds
5.52	MX	11.58pm	St Pancras-Bradford pcls
6.18		6.18am	Cudworth-Leeds*
6.46	MX	4.40am	Derby-Leeds parcels
7.23		7.23am	Cudworth-Leeds*
8s1		7.10am	Sheffield-Leeds
8.22		7.44am	Sheffield-Bradford #
9s27		8.40am	Sheffield-Cudworth DMU
9s48		6.42am	Birmingham-Bradford #
10.52		10.10	Sheffield-Bradford
pm			
12s23		11.38	Sheffield-Leeds DMU
12.48		7.40am	Bristol-Bradford
1.7		9.15am	St Pancras-Edinburgh # *The Waverley*
1s13		12.0	Sheffield-Leeds parcels
2.5pm		10.15am	St Pancras-Glasgow # *The Thames-Clyde Express*
3s18		2.31pm	Sheffield-Leeds *
4.2		12.15pm	St Pancras-Bradford #
		4.40pm	Royston-Normanton *(school days only)*
5s4		4.15pm	Sheffield-Leeds*
5.10	FO	4.25pm	Sheffield-Leeds *(Portion of 9.30 Bournemouth-Sheffield)*
5s37		9.15am	Paignton-Bradford # *The Devonian*
5.45	FO	5.0pm	Sheffield-Bradford ECS *(Until 15th July and on 9th Sept)*
6.7		2.15pm	St Pancras-Bradford #
6s18		5.28pm	Sheffield-Cudworth *
6.35		6.35pm	Cudworth-Royston loco LE *(Off 5.25 ex-Leeds. Via H&B line)*
7.21		3.15pm	St Pancras-Bradford #
8s17		7.27pm	Sheffield-Leeds *
9.1		5.6pm	St Pancras-Bradford
11s7		10.22pm	Sheffield-Leeds*

Up Direction

Time	Days	Dep.	Train
am			
12.44	MWO	6.38pm	Glasgow-Marylebone car sleeper
1.21	MX	12.25pm	Leeds-Bedford parcels
2.50	TFO	8.35pm	Stirling-Sutton Coldfield car sleeper
3.17		9.5pm	Glasgow-St Pancras
3.32		10.55pm	Carlisle-Sheffield parcels
4s1		3am	Leeds-Derby mail
4.24		10.5pm	Edinburgh-St Pancras #
4.51	MX	3.25am	Bradford-Derby ECS
7s30		6.37am	Leeds-Sheffield
8.10	MX	3.40am	Carlisle-Derby
8.17		7.12am	Bradford-St Pancras #
8s44		7.32am	Bradford-Bristol #
9s15		8.13am	Leeds-Sheffield
9.42	MX	8.58am	LE from Leeds
9.57		8.52am	Bradford-St Pancras#
10s5		10.5am	DMU to Sheffield
11.19		10.15am	Bradford-Paignton # *The Devonian*
11.39		10.30am	Bradford-St Pancras #
pm			
1.10		12.0	Bradford-St Pancras #
2s0		1.17pm	Leeds-Sheffield DMU
2.52	MFO	9am	Glasgow-St Pancras *(From 4th July)*
3.8		9.20am	Glasgow-St Pancras *The Thames Clyde Express*
3.49		12.42pm	Carlisle-Sheffield # *(22nd July-19th August)*
4.5		10.5am	Edinburgh-St Pancras # *The Waverley*
5s8		4.15pm	Leeds-Sheffield
5.56		4.45pm	Bradford-Bristol #
6s9		5.25pm	from Leeds
6s42		5.25pm	Bradford-Sheffield
7s6		6.20pm	from Leeds
7s15			ECS off the above to Heeley CS
7s59		6.5pm	Bradford-Derby
9s9	FO	8.20pm	Leeds-Sheffield
9.37	FO	8.25pm	Bradford-Bournemouth
9s39	FX	8.50pm	Leeds-Sheffield
9.57	FO	8.45pm	Bradford-Paignton
10.31		9.2pm	Bradford-Bristol #
11.4		9.30pm	Bradford-St Pancras
11.15		5.47pm	Carlisle-Cricklewood milk

**Accelerated timing s Calls at Cudworth*
 # ßpecial load limit/limited load

David Holmes was assistant area manager (movements) at Knottingley, including Cudworth, from the start of the area management organisation in February, 1970.

His responsibilities included safety of the line, visiting signal boxes, delivering notices and stores, checking train registers and seeing that duties were properly carried out. He also attended incidents and derailments.

"I don't think many people realise just how many minor derailments occurred in colliery sidings and BR yards, especially where track was not properly maintained.

"Carlton yards were very run down as closure had been planned since the opening of Healey Mills in 1963. I was often called out during the night to derailments there.

"Two enormous mishaps at Grimethorpe coalite plant were caused by rafts of loaded coal wagons getting away from the received sidings and running downhill for half a mile. One raft collided with a loaded train of coalite being propelled, resulting in a 20ft pile of mangled wagons, coal and coalite. Luckily nobody was hurt - in my experience they rarel;y were. I spent all night there while it was being sorted out. In the next sidings I could see loaded BR wagons glowing in the dark with hot coalite in them.

"One Sunday, three of four p way trains working in the Cudworth area were derailed. At Grimethorpe, a loco was rerailed by a notorious Holbeck tool vans supervisor who always left a big hole in the track. I ended up working single line by myself all night after the p way men went home in disgust.

"Another time, a bufferlocking at Carlton North led to 17 wagons all over the shop at Royston Junction, demolishing a lamp room, signals and mangling point rods. The C&W supervisor climbed the 20ft cutting side to put a 'Not to Go' card on a wheel-less 21-ton hopper. He once had a 'Not to Go' card put on my car when it got a flat tyre! In truth, we all worked together as a happy team.

"When a train divided on the Monk Bretton branch, it was a classic case of a coupling parting due to a heavy load on a steep bank. The guard then made the equally classic mistake of trying to recouple the train, succeeding only in pushing the rear half back down the hill where it derailed at the trap point.

"I used to spend alternate Saturday mornings in the former yard manager's dreary little office at Carlton, next to the H&B empty sidings and Britain's biggest bus scrap yard.

"At that time there were still four tracks on the main line but few passenger trains so the Fast lines were little used.

"The Monckton coking works sent a train of coke to ICI, Northwich nearly everyday. It was a family business and I once attended a meeting in the oak-panelled boardroom.

"Engineering work near Wath Road on Sunday 18th June, 1972 prevented passenger trains using the S&K line so they were diverted via Cudworth, giving us a preview of the resurgence soon to come. The 21 trains, most class 1, included five expresses between Leeds or Glasgow and St Pancras, news and parcels trains as well as North East-South West expresses and Sheffield-York DMUs."

On the morning of 18th August, 1971, David Holmes logged these trains at Cudworth

08.58 Class 45 No.143 on the Up Goods with 8V64 Carlton-West Drayton Coalite
09.05 Class 37 No.6938 on the Down Goods with 9K68 Grimethorpe-Carlton Nth
09.42 Class 37 No.6736 on the Down Goods with 9K67 Grimethorpe-Carlton Sth
09.52 Class 37 No.6938 on the Up Goods with 9K68 Carlton Nth-Grimethorpe slack
10.06 Class 31 No.5541 on the Up Goods with 9K53 Carlton Sth-Dearne Valley
10.13 Class 47 No.1878 on the Down Goods with 6K86 9.54 Grimethorpe-West Burton
10.36 Class 37 No.6736 on the Up Goods with 9K67 Carlton Sth-Grimethorpe slack
11.04 Class 37 No 6940 on the Up Goods with a Crofton Depot-Cudworth ballast
11.26 Class 31 No.5541 on the Down Goods with 9K53 Dearne Valley-Carlton Sth
11.33 Class 37 No.6938 on the Down Goods with 9K68 Grimethorpe-Carlton Sth
11.40 Class 40 No.348 on the Up Fast with 9J91 9.30 Crofton Depot-Beighton
11.54 Class 45 No.117 on the Down Goods with 6E11
12.01 Class 37 No.6736 on the Down Goods with 9K67 Grimethorpe-Carlton Sth
12.03 Class 47 No.1547 on the Up Fast with 8E20 the 05.20 Carlisle-Tinsley
12.10 Class 46 No.171 on the Up Slow for 9M10 the 12.43 Carlton-Toton
12.16 Class 47 No.1518 on the Down Slow with 1Z00 empty Inter-City stock
12.17 Class 25 No.7501 on the Up Fast with 6M84 the 7.35am Carlisle-Nottingham

Above: Ex-NER D20/2 4-4-0 No. 62360 was a rare visitor to Cudworth when it arrived on a mid-1950s railtour.. It created a wonderfully vintage scene with ex-Midland 1P 0-4-4T No. 58040 propelling the push-pull from Barnsley Court House into the station. *(Jim Davenport)*

When the locomotive of a train stood in the Up Fast or Up Slow platforms has to run round its train via South Junction signal box, or another locomotive has to be placed at the rear of a train or vehicle detached from a train...the guard or shunter must go toward South Junction box to meet the locomotive and conduct it to the rear of the train. In fog or falling snow the guard or shunter must conduct the locomotive from South Junction box. *Eastern Region(Northern Area) Sectional Appendix, 1968.*

Below: Ivatt class 2 2-6-2T No. 41281 waits to leave Cudworth with the 'Pusha ' to Barnsley Court House shortly before the service was withdrawn in 1958. Moving forwards, in a northerly direction, it would take the South West leg of the Cudworth triangle to reach the Court House branch. *(N. E. Stead Collection)*

SHORT MEMORIES

3.11.62: Black Five 44694 works the last Halifax-St Pancras.

Spring 1963: A new NE Region freight strategy for completion of the big marshalling yards foresees retention of Carlton and Cudworth yards to feed Eggborough power station.

April, 1965: Class 40 diesels on Healey Mills-Barnsley clearance tests and crew training runs.

Above: Monk Bretton was the only station between Cudworth and Barnsley and even then it closed on 27th September, 1937. This was how it looked around the early 20th century. *(Lens of Sutton)*

Wagons detached in Messrs Nicholson's sidings must be secured by sprags. The scotch blocks must be placed across the railway and the gate closed. *Eastern Region(Northern Area) Sectional Appendix, 1968*

Below: The lofty latticework of 1,087ft-long Oaks Viaduct makes a truly awe-inspiring sight as Ivatt 2-6-2T No. 41274 rumbles across with 'The Pusha ' towards Cudworth in the mid-1950s. A hundred or so feet below in the Dearne Valley are the two legs of the Barnsley Coal Railway which will meet at Oakwell Junction further to the left. In the foreground is the line from Stairfoot while the line from Barnsley runs along another elevated structure. *(Kenneth Field)*

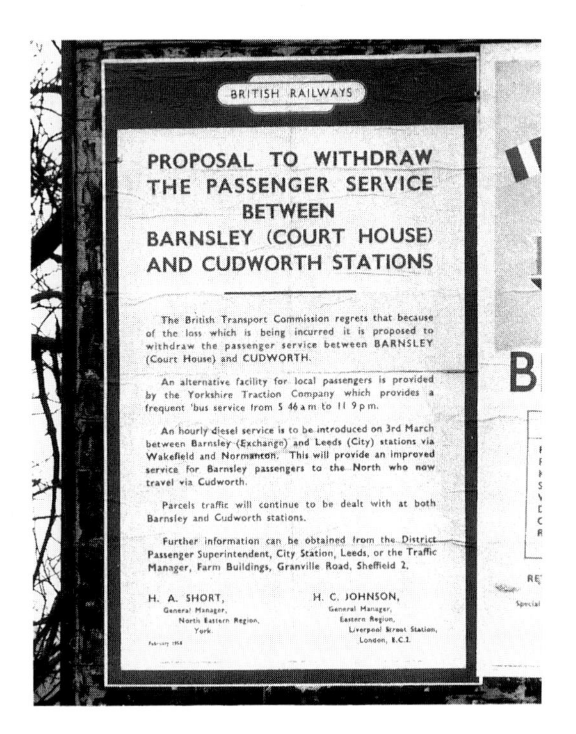

BRITISH RAILWAYS
PROPOSAL TO WITHDRAW
THE PASSENGER SERVICE
BETWEEN
BARNSLEY (COURT HOUSE)
AND CUDWORTH STATIONS
The British Transport Commission regrets that because of the loss which is being incurred it is proposed to withdraw the passenger service between BARNSLEY (Court House) and CUDWORTH.
An alternative facility for local passengers is provided by the Yorkshire Traction Company which provides a frequent 'bus service from 5 46 a m to 11 9 p m.
An hourly diesel service is to be introduced on 3rd March between Barnsley (Exchange) and Leeds (City) stations via Wakefield and Normanton. This will provide an improved service for Barnsley passengers to the North who now travel via Cudworth.
Parcels traffic will continue to be dealt with at both Barnsley and Cudworth stations.
Further information can be obtained from the District Passenger Superintendent, City Station, Leeds, or the Traffic Manager, Farm Buildings, Granville Road, Sheffield 2.
H. A. SHORT,
General Manager,
North Eastern Region,
York.
H. C. JOHNSON,
General Manager,
Eastern Region,
Liverpool Street Station,
London, E.C.2.

Above: The poster announcing withdrawal of the Barnsley-Cudworth service also hails the coming of diesel trains between Barnsley, Wakefield and Leeds on 3rd March, 1958. *(David Green)*

In summer, 1957, the 'Pusha' left Cudworth at 5.55am, 7.0am, 7.45, 8.27(SO), 9.2, 11.56(SO), 1.44pm, 2.55(WSO), 4.43(SO), 5.24(SO), 5.26(SX), 9.24, 10.5(SO) and 11.10(SO), and Barnsley Court House at 4.25am, 8.12(SO), 8.48, 9.29, 9.58, 2.16pm, 3.17(WO),3.22(SO), 5.10(SO) 5.48, 6.22(SX), 6.46(SO), and 9.50. The journey time was 10 minutes from Barnsley and 11 minutes from Cudworth. A reduced service ran on Sundays.

The service was axed in 1958 , the section over Oaks viaduct from Monk Bretton to Oaks Colliery being lifted early in 1960.

From then on, just 1,276 yards of the 4.25-mile Cudworth-Barnsley line remained in use. Still double track, it climbed at 1 in 75 to Monk Bretton sidings, had a top speed of 20mph and permissive block signalling between Cudworth North Junction and Monk Bretton signal boxes.

Booked trains were the 6.30am (SX) class F from Waterloo Colliery Sidings (Leeds), whose engine and brake van returned to Carlton South at 8.30; and the daily Normanton 66 trip which arrived around 9.25am, shunting until about 10.50 before returning to Carlton South.

By 1968, the line had been singled and was worked under One Engine in Steam regulations with no Train Staff.

It survives to carry the only Barnsley area freight traffic in 1996, a bulk sand train from Norfolk booked to reach to the Redfearn Glass works at around 16.00 on Mondays to Fridays but which actually runs as required.

Below: BR Standard class 2 2-6-2T No. 84009 pushes a Cudworth-bound train away from Barnsley between Court House and West Junction. The Mexborough line is down on the right. *(Kenneth Field)*

Left: The H&B platform at Cudworth with its simple but stylish building in 1952, its tracks occupied by coal wagons.The Midland main line, looking north, and Cudworth South Junction signal box are in the background. *(Richard Morton collection/ Barnsley Library)*

The H&B line from Hull ended at Stairfoot Junction while goods lines continued from Cudworth Yard South to Cudworth South Junction where they joined the Midland main line.

Freight only since 1932, the surviving main and goods lines still used absolute block signalling as late as 1968, even though the main line had closed altogether beyond Monckton Empty Sidings.

Maximum speed on the main lines between Cudworth Yard South and Monckton in 1968 was 40mph with 15mph on through sidings, and 30mph on the goods lines to Cudworth South Junction.

H&B signal boxes were at Cudworth Yard South, 3 miles from Stairfoot and 1,320 yards from Cudworth South Junction, Cudworth Yard North, 1,432 yards from Yard South, and, after 1,715 yards, Monckton Empty Sidings.

The new Cudworth Station Stairfoot line created in 1967 was 2 miles 178 yards long, had permissive block signalling, a maximum speed of 25mph and a 1 in 380 falling gradient from Cudworth.

Below: At Cudworth Yard South Junction on 6th June, 1962 8F 2-8-0 No.48466 hauls a load of empties from the storage sidings, situated between the H&B and Midland lines, past one of a few H&B signals remaining in the area. Fitted with a low level repeater, this one was deemed unsafe and replaced before the end of the year. *(Peter Rose)*

Platelayers take a break as 8F No.48093 rushes the bank with a special trip to Hemsworth Exchange Sidings on 1st June, 1962. The picture was taken from the steps of Cudworth Yard North signal box, the H&B yard being on the right. *(Peter Rose)*

Cudworth H&B Yard Departures and Arrivals

2nd November, 1959 - 12th June, 1960

DEPARTURES

6.45am		Class H	to Upton & North Elmsall
7.25am		Class K	to Wrangbrook
7.45am		Class F	to Wrangbrook
8.25am		Class F	to Wrangbrook
11am	SX	Class F	to Wrangbrook
11.30am		Class J	to Wrangbrook
12noon	FSX	Class F	to Wrangbrook
12.35pm		Class F	to Upton & North Elmsall

ARRIVALS

10.15am		10am	Engine and brake van from Hemsworth Sdgs.
11.5am		10.35 am	Class H from Wrangbrook
11.45am		11.15am	Class H from Wrangbrook
1.42pm	SX	1.22pm	Engine and brake van from Wrangbrook
2.20pm	FSX	1.57pm	Engine and brake van from Wrangbrook
2.30pm		2.10pm	Class H from Upton & North Elmsall
2.30pm		1.25pm	Class K from Wrangbrook
2.45pm	SO	2.22pm	Class J from Wrangbrook
3.40pm	SX	3.10pm	Class J from Wrangbrook

SHORT MEMORIES

1.5.65: 8F 48337 passes Royston pushing independant snowplough No. DB965225 en-route to Skipton.

13.9.65: Crigglestone and Haigh stations closed.

9.10.65: Ivatt 2-6-0s 43076-9 and WDs 90318/37 transfer to Royston.

An electric gong operated by guards or shunters was available at Cudworth Yard North to assist the shunting of trains from the Up main to the storage sidings, signalling go ahead, stop, set back or ease couplings.

Cudworth motive power depot was established along with the Hull and Barnsley complex in 1885 and for nearly 50 years was the only shed in the vicinity. It consisted of an eight-road shed with northlight roof, and the usual facilities including a 50 ton capacity mechanical coaling plant, water tower, a 60ft turntable and a set of shearlegs.
Under British Railways, Cudworth was coded 53E in the North Eastern Region's Hull district, having been a part of the NE system since being taken over by its arch rival, the North Eastern Railway, in 1922.
When Cudworth and the neighbouring LMS shed at Royston came under the single authority of BR upon nationalisation in 1948, the need for two sheds within a stone's throw of each other quickly diminished. This and the continuing decline of traffic on the H&B hastened Cudworth shed's downfall and it closed in July, 1951.
In the 1920s, around 30 engines were allocated to Cudworth .Towards the end, its fleet was entirely GC or NE in origin, the 0-6-0, 0-8-0 and 0-6-2Ts of the H&B having been mostly phased out during the 1930s. By 1949 Cudworth's allocation consisted of two ex-NE Q5 0-8-0s, three ex-GC O4 2-8-0s, three ex-NE J25 0-6-0s and two ex-NE A7 4-6-2Ts. Upon closure, the O4s went to ex-LMS Royston shed until it could get rid of them - at least one said to have ended up in the Middle East during the Suez crisis.
Above: By the time this picture was taken in 1950, half the shed had lost its roof and was occupied by cold and inactive A7 No. 69771. *(N. E. Stead collection)*

LOCOMOTIVES ALLOCATED TO CUDWORTH

August 1950: O4 2-8-0: 63620/67/751/843/9; J25 0-6-0: 65714. Total: 6

The winter 1959/60 Working Timetable showed the following booked west and southbound trains from Cudworth yard: 7.55am Class J to Mottram, 8.20am Class J to Mottram, 10.15am Class H to Stanton Works, Ilkeston, 11.15am Class J to Wath Yard, 11.45am Class J to Mottram, 3.30pm Class J to Mottram. Incoming trains, showing arrival times, were: 6.57am Class J from Wath Yard, 7.45am light engine from Barnsley Top Yard, 9.35am light engine from Mexborough MPD with brake van from Stairfoot and light engine from Wombwell Exchange(both engines coupled together), 1.20pm Class J from Storrs Mill, 1.34pm Class J from Wath Yard, 5.50pm Class J from Wath Yard, 6.30pm Class J from Storrs Mill.

Above: Ex-Midland 4F No. 43983 is well stoked up for its attack on the 1 in 100 climb from Cudworth Yard to Monckton Empty Sidings with wagons for the coke works on 1st June, 1962. The nearest cableway pylon marks the start of a new spoil tip for Monckton Colliery.

The NE Region 1960 Sectional Appendix gave the following instruction about the working of empty wagons up the bank to the Empty Coke Siding at Monckton Main:...when wagons are propelled up the incline to the coke empty sidings by BR locomotives, the locomotive or locomotives must... be chimney first and the number of wagons must not exceed 15....Should the BR locomotive be tender first not more than 10 wagons... may be propelled at any one time. Only one locomotive, or two locomotives coupled together, must be allowed on the incline between the hand points in the Inwards Coke Road and the Empty Coke Sidings, at one time.

Below: LMS-built 4F No. 44446 works hard pushing empties up the branch from Monckton Empty Sidings to the coke works on 6th June, 1962. *(Both Peter Rose)*

Above: Monckton Empty Sidings was where the Lancashire & Yorkshire's Dearne Valley Junction line from Crofton to the Dearne Valley proper at Shafton Junction crossed over the Hull and Barnsley. On a September, 1962 day, Royston's ex-Midland 4F No. 43906 was standing by the signal box while a workstained WD 2-8-0 from Wakefield headed a train of empties over the top towards Grimethorpe. No. 43906 still had LMS on the tender with the early BR lion and wheel stamped over the 'M'. *(Peter Rose)*

Below: Hughes-Fowler 'Crab' 2-6-0 No. 42762 drifts down from Brierley Junction towards Cudworth on 4th September, 1962. On the left is the line at Monckton Empty Sidings where empty wagons were reversed before being propelled up to the coking works. It could accommodate 58 wagons, engine and brake van. *(Peter Rose)*

Above: 4F No. 44290 clatters over the points at Brierley Junction and heads for Cudworth with a delightfully mixed pick-up goods including pulverite and Presflo wagons. This was the starting point of the Dearne Valley Railway which curves towards us and joins the L&Y line from Crofton 1,071 yards further on at Shafton Junction. *(Peter Rose)*

The 1960 NE Region Sectional Appendix stated that an electric bell was provided at Brierley empty sidings to assist drivers and guards with shunting movements necessitating drawing onto the Up and Down through siding towards Shafton.

Below: The Brierley Junction to Shafton Junction curve was worked as through sidings limited to 10mph. This view looking towards Brierley on 31st May, 1962 shows Wakefield WD 2-8-0 No. 90342 and a 4F in attendance. The Dearne Valley is behind the fence on the left. *(Peter Rose.)*

The lines between Brierley Junction and Shafton signal boxes are not worked under any Block system. A stop signal, worked by Shafton, controlling entrance to the Up and Down through siding is provided at the Brierley end of this siding.

A miniature distant signal acting as repeater and worked from Shafton is situated 256 yards behind the Shafton home signal. This repeater is provided with a board showing a black "R" on a yellow background.....

Through movements from Brierley to Shafton must use the Up through siding...

All movements along the Up and Down through siding from the Shafton end must be brought to a stand at the stop board next to the first pair of spring assisted hand points giving admission to Brierley Sidings..the driver will be responsible for ensuring that the two sets of points are correctly set...

Through movements from Shafton to Brierley must use the Down through siding between the stop board and Brierley. *NER Sectional Appendix* 1960

In 1960 there were signal boxes in the area of the Dearne Valley covered by this book at Shafton Junction (4 miles 999 yards from Crofton Hall), Grimethorpe Sidings (2 miles 730 yards from Shafton), and Houghton Sidings (968 yards).

Signalling was absolute block from Crofton to Shafton with permissive block for goods trains beyond there - absolute block applying if Crofton South, Crofton Hall or Shafton boxes were closed. Maximum speed was 45mph.

The new junction with the Midland, commissioned on 11th July, 1966, was Dearne Valley North, the Goldthorpe portion leaving the remaining 2 mile 1160-yard stub to Grimethorpe at Dearne Valley South. Both junctions were operated from Cudworth Station box. No boxes remained on the DV which had no block signalling.

In summer 1965 the only booked train on the DV, was OK55, the Thursday 11.30 Crofton Hall to Goldthorpe engine and brake van which delivered wages. All other trains were trips working as required.

Above: With Grimethorpe Colliery sidings below left and the muck stack towering above, WD 2-8-0 No. 90635 moves a heavy coal train for Crofton along the Dearne Valley in June, 1961. Just visible is Grimethorpe Sidings signal box which was renamed Grimethorpe South six months later. *(David Green)*

Below: Climbing the 1 in 100 to Ryhill while on its way to Crofton with coal from one of the Dearne Valley collieries, WD No. 90651 on a Wakefield bonus turn thunders over the H & B at Monckton Empty Sidings, 1st September, 1962. *(Peter Rose)*

A Cravens (later class 105) diesel multiple unit from Leeds to Sheffield leaves Haigh station on 2nd November, 1963.
On Mondays to Fridays during summer, 1957, Haigh was served by nine steam trains to Barnsley, eight to Wakefield and one to Goole.
It closed to passengers on 13th September, 1965 and to goods on 6th July, 1964. *(David Green)*

BARNSLEY EXCHANGE AND THE LANKY

In 1960 the Barnsley-Horbury line had stations at Darton, Haigh and Crigglestone West, signal boxes at Barnsley Exchange Junction, Silkstone Junction, Darton, Woolley Coal Siding, Haigh, and Crigglestone Junction, and absolute block signalling. No maximum line speed was defined so drivers were instructed not to exceed 60mph.

Barnsley Exchange was served on Mondays to Fridays by 12 Leeds City-Sheffield DMUs each way plus a few extras to and from Wakefield and one to Bradford Exchange via Wakefield. The first train into Barnsley was the 5.40am arrival from Wakefield and the first departure the 6.10am return(neither shown as a DMU in the working timetable). A summer Saturday Blackpool train left at 8.35am, returning at 4.32pm. Empty stock came from and went back to Wakefield.

The 8.44am Halifax portion of the St Pancras train called at Barnsley at 9.52am, and returned at 9.7pm. On summer Saturdays it ran as a seperate through train on slightly different timings.

By summer 1965, loco-hauled trains included the Friday 20.20 Bradford Forster Square-Bournemouth(16.7-13.8), leaving Barnsley at 21.54. The 01.17 1E40 Manchester Piccadilly-Cleethorpes called at Barnsley 02.25-02.29.

The 1959/60 working timetable showed 15 booked freights in the Down(Horbury) direction and 21 on the Up plus numerous engine and brake van movements. Most trains were loaded or empty trips between Darton or Woolley collieries and Wath yard, Stairfoot, Healey Mills, Mirfield and Wakefield, but they included a 9.30am Godley Junction - Darton class J and a Monday 7.25am Barrow-in-Furness-Wath class F.

Mining subsidence caused Darton station to be rebuilt twice. The first time was in 1960 after the original platforms had sunk so low that they were replaced by this timber structure, seen looking towards Barnsley on 3rd February, 1961. With coal mining gone, and subsidence ended, they have now been rebuilt in concrete. The box, colliery connections and sidings have all gone. *(By courtesy of British Rail)*

Top: Darton station on 16th May, 1981 with class 31 No. 31256. The Barnsley platform was reached by crossing the siding on the right.

Centre: Between Haigh and Darton was Woolley colliery, the source of much Wakefield-Barnsley line freight until the 1980s. This 0-6-0 diesel, built in 1968 by Hunslet of Leeds, was shunting the yard on 22nd March, 1974. The Hunslet works closed in 1995 but its industrial locomotive operation continues at the Qualter Hall factory, Summer Lane, Barnsley.

Bottom: The NCB line to North Gawber colliery left the main line at Darton . It was one of the last outposts of steam with an Austerity 0-6-0ST covering for diesel breakdowns until the mid-1970s. Hunslet 3212, built 1945, hauls a long line of empties up to the pit on 4th June,1971.
(All Adrian Booth)

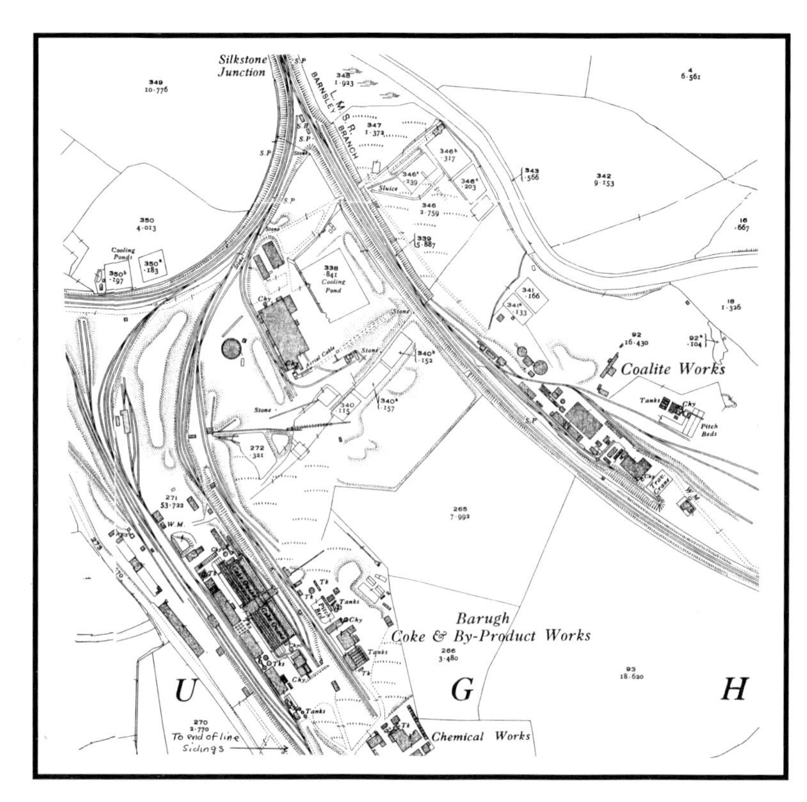

SHORT MEMORIES

April, 1966: A half-mile section of line between Summer Lane and Dodworth is singled and realigned to make room for the M1.

July, 1966: Royston shed receives an influx of WDs, Nos. 90054/615/ 42/721 from Wakefield.

Summer, 1966: Jubilee No. 45562 *Alberta* is regular power on the Bradford-Poole express but 45647 *Sturdee* works it on 2nd July and 45581 *Bihar and Orissa* on the 16th.

Above: Over its lifetime the Silkstone branch served about a dozen private sidings including Stanhope Colliery and the Barugh Green coke and byproducts works, shown on this reproduction of a 1934 1 in 2500 Ordnance Survey map. *(By courtesy of the Ordnance Survey)*

Below: The NCB shunter in boiler suit, waistcoat, trilby and bicycle clips, shouts orders to the BR crew of ex-L&Y Barton-Wright 2F 0-6-0 No. 52044 during operations at Barugh coke ovens on 11th September, 1953.The two tank cars are class A tanks for low flash point liquids, probably Benzole. Nearly all trace of this line has gone but in autumn, 1995 the engine was still pulling wagons along the preserved East Lancashire Railway. *(F. W. Shuttleworth)*

Above: Classic LNER power on the Lanky - J39 0-6-0 No. 64902 climbs the 1 in 102 Willow Bank on the approach to Barnsley with a coal train. in the 1950s. *(B.A.Jordan)*

Below: Class 04/8 2-8-0 No. 63726(rebuilt from 04/5 in 1958) contributes to a wonderful 1950s scene while clanking through Barnsley Exchange station with a northbound train of empties. The engine shed stands above the first two wagons while the goods yard on the right looks busy enough. It closed on 4th January, 1971 and, like the site of the engine shed, is now occupied by bus stands. *(Kenneth Field)*

The whole of Barnsley seems to have turned out to see the world's most famous locomotive visit Exchange station. No wonder, preserved LNER class A3 Pacific No. 4472 *Flying Scotsman* brought some cheer to the immediate post-steam and post-Beeching era when it arrived with a railtour on 21st June, 1969. The train travelled from Manchester via Woodhead, being hauled through the tunnel by an electric loco with '*Scotsman*' in light steam. Towards the back of the train is Barnsley Exchange Junction signal box, renamed Barnsley Station Junction in 1972, where the Penistone line diverges. *(Adrian Booth)*

Summer Saturdays at Exchange.
Above: Having arrived at 12.54pm on 26th August, 1961 with the 9.32am extra from Skegness, J11 0-6-0 No. 64442 and K3 2-6-0 No. 61943 are ready to take the empty stock away towards the Penistone line. In spite of all the other changes, the splitting signal was still being used in 1996. *(David Holmes)*

Below: The Bradford Exchange-Poole express was one of the most celebrated trains anywhere during the summers of 1965 and 66, not least because it was hauled by some of the last Jubilees and on alternate Saturdays consisted of Southern Region green coaches. In 1966 it was regularly hauled by No. 45562 *Alberta*, seen coming over Jumble Lane crossing into Exhange station with the corresponding return service on 20th August. Above the train are the redundant arches of the approach to Court House station. *(D.P. Leckonby/N.E.Stead collection)*

The exterior of Exchange station as it was in November, 1986, its dark entrance having changed little over the years. Seven years later it had all gone, replaced by the new interchange. *(Malcolm Roughley)*

Barnsley engine shed was a dream for enthusiasts, being on full view from the Exchange station platform and, being a mixed passenger and goods shed, it always displayed a varied selection of engines. It was originally shared with the L&Y but after that company's successor, the LMS, moved out, it became a stronghold of classic Great Central power to the end. Under BR, Barnsley was coded 36D in the Eastern Region's Doncaster district until 1958 when it became 41G in the Sheffield district. It closed in January, 1960 and was demolished straight away to make room for the station's new Sheffield platform.

LOCOMOTIVES ALLOCATED TO BARNSLEY: AUGUST, 1950

Q4 0-8-0: 63201/3/20/9/35; O4 2-8-0: 63623/97/727/883/904/13; J11 0-6-0: 64290/ 343/62/6 /91/8/9/ 425/36/48/52; C13 4-4-2T: 67409/11/34; N5 0-6-2T: 69268/78/85/91/303/20/5/34/458/55/7/65/7/8. Total: 40

Below: How we yearn for a filthy, smoky scene like this. Seen from the footbridge at Jumble Lane in the late 1950s, it shows J11 0-6-0 No. 64404 nearest the camera, a selection of O4s, the two-road shed, coaler, and the sort of level crossing gates we all loved to hang around at as grubby youngsters clutching dog-eared notebooks. The whole area is now occupied by the transport interchange and buses stand where the engines were. *(N.E.Stead collection)*

Great Central heritage at Barnsley shed in the 1950s. Right: Among the fine show of pre-grouping engines to be seen there were the Q4 0-8-0s like No. 63220. Designed by J.G. Robinson, it was built in 1904 by Kitsons of Leeds.
(Peter Hughes)

Left: They might look antique nowadays but the C14 Atlantic tanks were the mainstay of local passenger services. Nos. 67447 and 67448 grace the loco yard on 23rd March, 1958 with Jumble Lane crossing and railway houses behind. Also a Robinson design, they were built in 1907.
(David Holmes)

Right: The class N5 0-6-2Ts were the oldest of this lot, being introduced by the Manchester, Sheffield and Lincolnshire Railway in 1891 to the design of T. Parker. No. 69320 stands in the yard amid the J11s and C14s at 2.43pm on 23rd March, 1958.
(David Holmes)

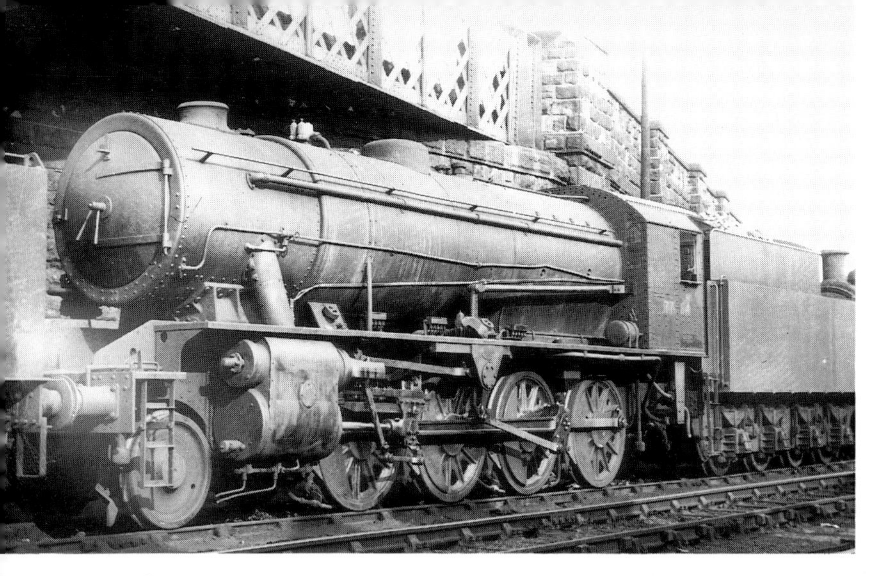

Top: Built for the war effort, the WD 2-8-0s were common enough but in 1947 Barnsley shed had five or six still carrying War Department numbers. No. 77484 was stabled beneath the girder bridge carrying the eastern approach to Court House station. The sidings here were used as an overspill for the shed. *(Ken Boulter)*

Centre: Barnsley West Junction (left) and Pinder Oaks signal boxes, seen looking east, controlled the parallel Sheffield (Midland) and Mexborough (GC) lines. *(David Green)*

Bottom: Barnsley's own class O4/3 2-8-0 No. 63883 makes a stirring sight while hauling wagons loaded with timber past Freeman's coal yard in Pontefract Road and towards the girder bridge. These engines were built in 1917 for the first world war effort. The Midland line to Court House is up on the left. *(Kenneth Field)*

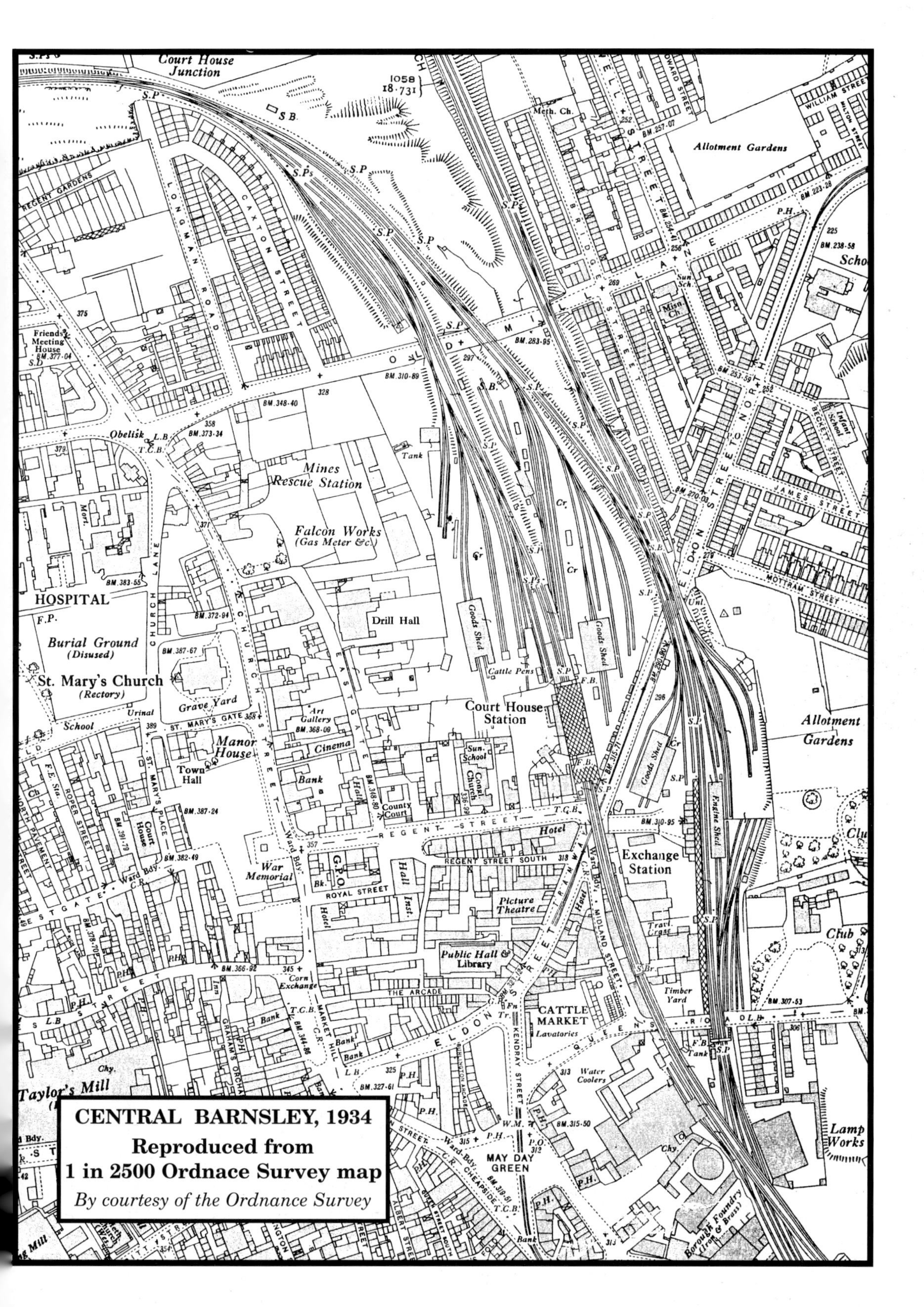

CENTRAL BARNSLEY, 1934
Reproduced from
1 in 2500 Ordnace Survey map
By courtesy of the Ordnance Survey

COURT HOUSE, SHEFFIELD & PENISTONE

Abve: Local trains from Barnsley ended their journeys in the back platform at Penistone, clear of the electrified Manchester-Sheffield main line. Beautifully groomed C13 4-4-2T No. 67434 stands beneath the 1500 volt DC wires before returning to Barnsley. (*N.E.Stead collection)*

Below: One Sunday every month during the 1950s summers a Blackpool-Doncaster excursion ran via Barnsley. This May, 1959 view shows the train descending from West Silkstone Junction behind Blackpool Black Five 4-6-0 No. 44947. The electrified Worsborough branch approaches on the left. *(Peter Sunderland).*

In 1968 the maximum speed on main lines between New Oaks Jn. and West Silkstone Jn. was 40mph. Signalling was absolute block with mainly permissive block on goods lines. Signal boxes were New Oaks Jn., Stairfoot Jn., Quarry Jn., Jumble Lane, Barnsley Exchange Jn., Court House Jn., Summer Lane, Dodworth, and West Silkstone Jn. The Exchange Down platform was signalled in both directions.

Up and Down goods lines ran between New Oaks and Stairfoot, an Up refuge siding at Exchange Jn. held 60 wagons, engine and brake van, and a Down refuge siding at West Silkstone 26 wagons, engine and brake.

Trains faced a 10-mile slog, starting with 1 in 118 to Stairfoot, then 1 in 62/68 to Quarry Jn., a brief 1 in 160 down to Jumble Lane, then 1 in 41/50 to Dodworth and 1 in 100 to Penistoe.

Above: A bit blurred it may be but what a classic. A not quite identifiable ex-GC D9 4-4-0 and a 4-4-2T thrash towards West Silkstone Junction with a Penistone stopper. The D9 is in wartime livery with NE on the tender and pre-1946 LNER number. *(Ken Boulter)*

The Eastern Region(South) 1968 Sectional Appendix stated that locomotives, not coupled to the train, could provide rear end assistance to freight trains between Wombwell Central and Barnsley Exchange Jn., Stairfoot Jn. and New Oaks Jn.(in clear weather only), Stairfoot Jn. and W. Silkstone Jn. via Barnsley, Stairfoot Jn. and Wharncliffe Woodmoor, and between Cudworth and Stairfoot where assisting engines may be coupled.

Below: N5 0-6-2T No. 69325 was sporting lined black livery instead of more usual plain black when it was banking an unfitted goods up to West Silkstone Junction in the 1950s. *(Peter Hughes)*

Above: The 23rd May, 1959 was a pleasantly sunny day even though the cold wind of change was blowing. J11 0-6-0 No. 64404 rolls past the quite remarkable Silkstone signalbox and into the station with the 4.50pm Penistone-Mexborough.

Below: Looking the other way on the same day, with C14 No. 67445 on a Penistone-bound train. The Barnsley-Penistone local service was withdrawn on 29th June but reinstated in May, 1983. A new Silkstone station was opened in 1984 with a timber platform on the remaining single track. *(Both David Holmes)*

Above: The usual J11 had given way to a more modern J39 0-6-0 for the 10.40am Barnsley-Penistone, pictured at Dodworth station on 14th February, 1959. *(P.B.Booth / N.E.Stead collection)*

Below: By then well away from the view of passengers, steam was still alive and well on BR at Dodworth well into the 1970s. On 18th September, 1972, 1943-built NCB Hunslet Austerity 0-6-0ST No. 2857(another type built for the war effort) was going through the everyday shunting routine of hauling merry-go-round wagons out of the colliery and on to the BR main line. *(Adrian Booth)*
The original signal box was destroyed by a pile-up of coal wagons in 1955, signalman Harry Falkner being lucky to get out alive.

SHORT MEMORIES

Mid-1966: Mining subsidence has slowed Leeds-Sheffield express journey times to 71 minutes compared with 49 minutes in 1939.

30.7.66: Jubilee 45562 *Alberta* slips to a halt with the Poole-Bradford while climbing the 1 in 50 out of Barnsley. A Brush Type 2 diesel provides assistance from the rear.

28.1.67: Engines transferred to Royston are 2-6-4Ts 42141/ 689(ex-Huddersfield) 8Fs 48084/93/126/30/622/ 703 (ex-Stourton); WDs 90649/ 80/94 (ex-Wakefield) and diesel shunters D2246/63 (ex-Huddersfield

Above: Summer Lane station was less than a mile from the main Barnsley stations but up a ferrocious curving 1 in 41/50 gradient which taxed engines and men in steam days. B1 4-6-0 No. 61112 from Mexborough shed sets off for Penistone with the 3pm from Cleethorpes in the 1950s, a train regularly used by Barnsley spotters on their way home after a day's seeking out more glamorous engines at Doncaster. *(David Green)*

Below: Summer Lane station on 17th June, 1961, still tidy despite being closed for two years. Looking towards Penistone, the large building is the Co-op warehouse. Barnsley was Britain's biggest Co-op then and received all kinds of goods and foodstuffs by rail, while wagons fill the coal yard which stayed in use until the 1970s. The MSL signalbox stands beyond them. *(H.B.Priestley / Howard Turner collection)*

In 1946, LNER trains left Barnsley Court House for Penistone at 6.38am, 8.10am (both from Mexborough), 1.20pm(SO), 2.18, 4.10, 6.11 (3pm ex-Grimsby), 10.16 (ex-Doncaster). The 7.5-mile all stations slog took 25 minutes. Missing Summer Lane, the 10.16 took 23 minutes.

Trains the other way were the 2.43am Penistone-Doncaster, 7.23am Penistone-Lincoln, 9.20am Penistone-Mexborough, the 1.35pm Penistone-Barnsley, 4.58pm Penistone-Mexborough and 6.27pm Penistone-Doncaster. Penistone-Barnsley journey times varied from 13 to 20 minutes. Trains were all stations. The non-stop 2.43am took 15 minutes.

Above: Among trains eagerly awaited by Barnsley enthusiasts were the evening fish workings from Hull and Grimsby. Doncaster B1 No. 61247 *Lord Burghley* storms the bank to Summer Lane past Keir Street school with the 5.35pm Hull to Guide Bridge in summer, 1952. *(Les Nixon)*

Below: J11 0-6-0 No. 4294 has just left the sidings at Court House Junction and is waiting to enter the station to form what is probably the 5.5pm to Sheffield Victoria on 23rd August, 1947. The leading coach looks to be of North Eastern Railway pattern while the second is thought to be Great Eastern. Down below on the right can be glimpsed the box vans in Barnsley Central goods yard. *(D.L.Wilkinson)*

Top: The west end of Court House, often referred to as `Top Station' because of its higher level. The goods yard is on the left and Goods Junction signal box beyond. The full British Railways lettering on ex-Midland 1P 0-4-4T No. 58040, resting the Cudworth 'Pusha' in the bay, dates the scene around 1950. *((David Green)*

Centre: Central Goods, the GCR goods station, was sandwiched at a lower level between Court House and Exchange. It closed on 6th November, 1967 and this was how it looked on 19th April, 1970. *(M. A. King/ Barnsley Library)*

Bottom: The Midland goods depot at Court House on the same day. The Barnsley goods depots were replaced by a new central freight terminal in Sheffield and this one closed on 31st January, 1966. *(M. A King)*

Above: Barnsley's own C14 4-4-2T No. 67448, displaying painted 36D shedcode, waits in the bay at Court House before leaving for Penistone on 10th May, 1958. The push-pull for Cudworth stands in one of the main platforms. *(Howard Turner)*

Below: The trains have swapped platforms to make a delightful pairing of two ages of steam. The C14 design of 1907 and BR Standard class 2 2-6-2T No. 84009 of 1953. *(Howard Turner)*

Above: Class C13 4-4-2T No. 67434 waits to leave from under the original Court House overall roof with the 5.10pm to Sheffield Victoria on 5th December, 1953, the last local passenger train via the GC route. *(A.C.Gilbert)*

Below: The diesels move in - a Derby Works two-car set(later class 114), forms a service to Sheffield Midland. These 1956-built units remained on the Barnsley line until the late-1980s by which time they were the oldest DMUs on British Rail. *(N.E.Stead collection)*

By 1946 the LNER Barnsley Court House - Sheffield Victoria service was down to the bare minimum. Trains left Court House at 6am, 7.55am and 5.5pm, taking 52 minutes for the 18.25-mile journey. The only two trains from Sheffield arrived at 6.45am and 5.50pm having taken 53 minutes. All trains called at all remaining stations - Stairfoot, Dovecliffe for Worsborough, Birdwell & Hoyland Common, Chapeltown Central, Ecclesfield East, Grange Lane and Meadow Hall.

Above: Classic Midland at Court House - Nottingham-based 2P 4-4-0 No. 40542, a class dating originally from 1891, awaits departure towards Sheffield Midland. The station roof was replaced by canopies in 1956. *(Kenneth Field)*

Below: With the Court House rebuilding under way, more modern power in the shape of Hasland-based Ivatt class 2 2-6-0 No. 46500 awaits departure with a five-coach stopper, possibly to Chesterfield. The Cudworth train stands behind at the same platform. *(David Green)*

Above: This mishap occurred at Quarry Junction in April, 1955. C13 4-4-2T No. 67411 was sent to move empty loco coal wagons from Jumble Lane sidings but the passenger tank could not hold the load which pushed it back down to the junction where it collided with N5 No. 69368 Both engines were scrapped afterwards, repairs not being thought worthwhile.
The picture, looking east, gives a good view of the area, showing the Barnsley Main Colliery spoil tips, the Court House lines on the left embankment with the Midland line to Sheffield crossing over the bridge, and Quarry sidings on the right. WD 2-8-0 No. 90150 is on the Mexborough break-down crane and a B16 4-6-0 has what may possibly be the York crane. *(P.J.Lynch)*

Below: N5 0-6-2T No. 69268 made a delightfully vintage scene while waiting the signal on the Barnsley side of Stairfoot Junction. The viaduct carries the Cudworth to Monk Spring Junction line. *(N.E.Stead collection)*

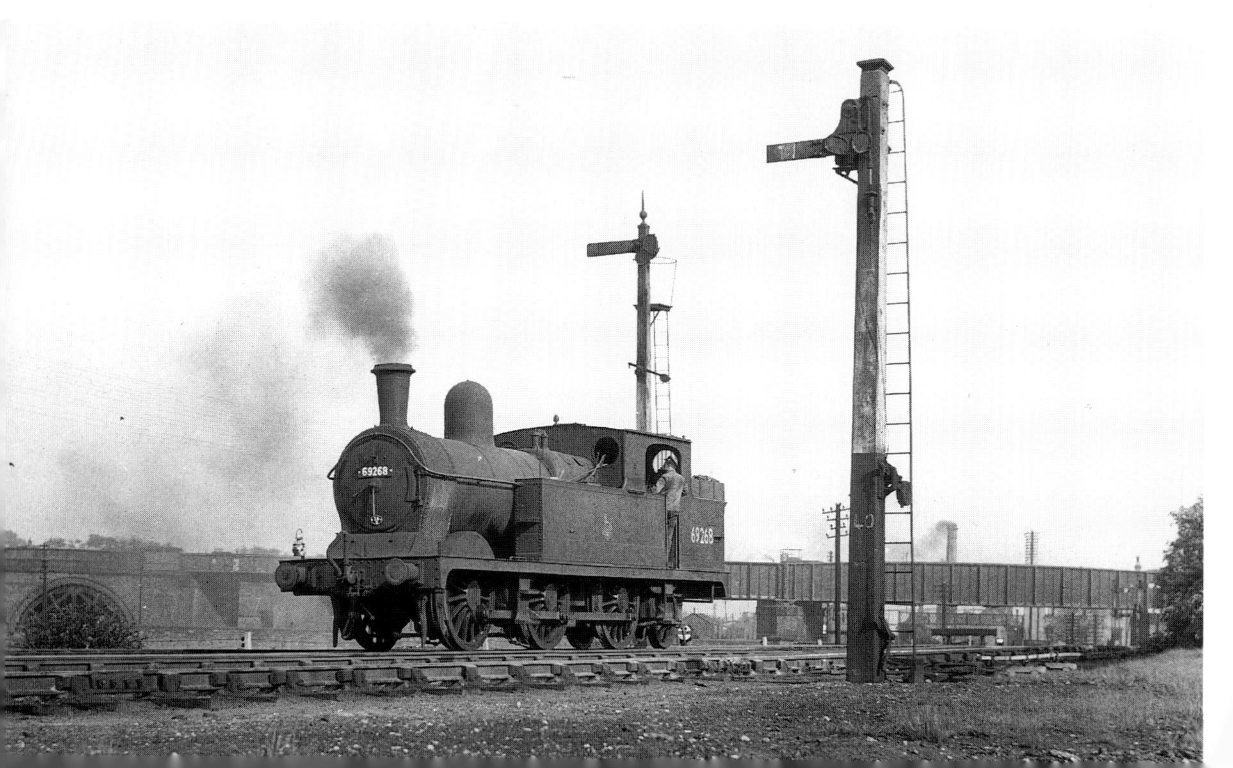

After withdrawal of the passenger service, the GC line to Sheffield remained in use for goods and special or diverted passenger trains until 1966. It was then severed between Birdwell and Chapeltown to save the cost of building a bridge for the new M1 motorway.

By 1968, just 3 miles 385 yards remained at its northern end, although it was still double track to Dovecliffe.

The line left the electrified Wath-Penistone branch at Wombwell Main Junction and terminated at a stop board at Rockingham South. On the way it served Barrow Colliery and coking works and Rockingham Colliery. Maximum line speed was 30mph with absolute block signalling as far as Dovecliffe, its only remaining signal box. The 2 miles 348 yards from there to Rockingham South were worked under One Engine in Steam regulations, meaning only one train on the line at a time.

The line remained in use until 1985 to serve Barrow Colliery, the coking works having closed in 1976 and Rockingham Colliery around 1978.

Above: Dovecliffe for Worsborough how it looked around the start of the 20th century, viewed towards Sheffield with buildings rather like a row of cottages and the bottom half of the signal box in the right foreground. *(Lens of Sutton)*

Below: Dovecliffe in August, 1973. The station has completely gone and the crossover is reversed, giving direct access to Barrow Colliery. The old 3-storey signal box still stands proud despite the new one which was commissioned in 1973. The Midland branch to Pilley and Wharncliffe ran behind the buildings on the right. The sand drag is just beyond the points. *(M.A.King/Barnsley Library)*

DOVECLIFFE STATION BOX - SAND DRAG: Facing points are laid in the single line 350 yards from the box, facing Up trains and leading to a sand drag interlaced in the single line.
All Up trains MUST be brought to a stand at the Dovecliffe station Up First Home signal, and until this has been done the sand drag points must be kept open......
BARROW COLLIERY SIDINGS: An engine or train must not be allowed to foul or pass the colliery company's connections leading from the colliery branch to the LMR line until the siding signal from the colliery, which normally stands in the 'off' position, has been placed to danger .....*(Eastern Region(Southern Area) Sectional Appendix, 1968. (It is assumed that the LMR line referred to a small remaining portion of the Wharncliffe branch)*

Left: It even looks like the end of the line. Rockingham South, its disused signal box and colliery sidings in April, 1979. *(M.A.King)*

Below: Birdwell and Hoyland Common station, Wharncliffe Silkstone Colliery and the end of the Wharncliffe branch as shown on a 1934 1 in 2500 Ordnance Survey map. *(By courtesy of the Ordnance Survey)*

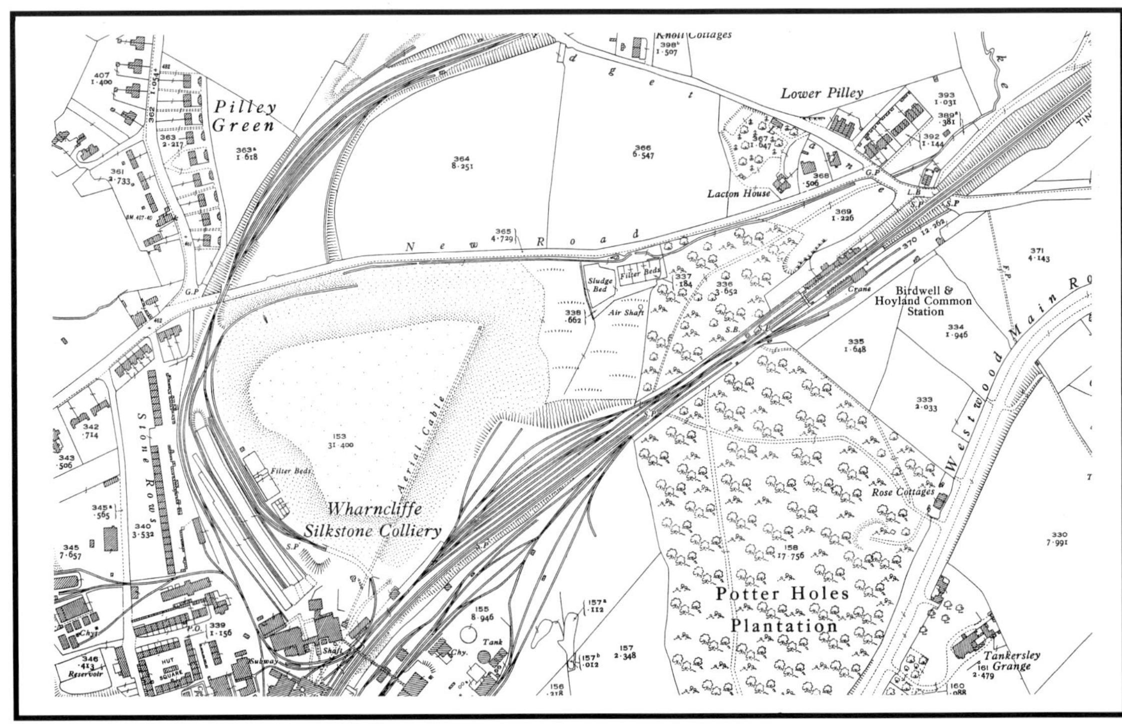

Right: Birdwell & Hoyland Common station looking towards Barnsley around the start of the 20th century. Birdwell closed to passengers on 7th December, 1953 and to goods on 2nd November, 1964.
(Howard Turner collection)

Having passed Wharncliffe Silkstone Colliery, the GC line curved round in an easterly direction into Westwood station. Beyond there were connections to Thorncliffe iron and chemical works.

Top: This was Westwood station in late Victorian times looking back towards Birdwell. The signal box, of usual MSLR style, competes very well with Dovecliffe for height. Westwood closed to passengers and goods on 28th October, 1940. *(Lens of Sutton)*

Centre: After crossing over the Midland Barnsley-Sheffield line above Tankersley Tunnel, the GC line swept into Chapeltown Central. Originally called Chapeltown, it was renamed Chapeltown and Thorncliffe when the Midland station opened in 1897, and Central in 1951. The station buildings are of a style to be found all over the MSL system. *(Lens of Sutton)*

Right: Chapeltown Central closed to passengers on 7th December, 1953 and goods on 1st April, 1955, but the yard was still occupied by wagons in 1962 when this picture was taken looking towards Sheffield. *(M.A.King)*

Above: The huge Smithywood coking works, between Chapeltown and Ecclesfield, kept the Sheffield end of the GC line and steam alive into the mid-1980s.
Taken from the footbridge over the works sidings, this 3rd November, 1975 view shows the remaining single track of the GC line which terminated just beyond the works, loaded coke wagons in the sidings, one the plant's two Austerity 0-6-0STs blowing off near the weighbridge, and the engine shed empty because the other 0-6-0ST was working on the coke car. *(Stephen Chapman)*

Below: An undated view, probably in the late 1940s, of a very well kept Ecclesfield East station. Ecclesfield East closed completely on 7th December, 1953, the goods yard becoming a scrap yard where several steam locomotives were broken up. *(B.N.Collins)*

SHORT MEMORIES

11.3.67: Brush Type 4 diesel No. D1546 hauls a special train from Barnsley to Wembley for a hockey international.

25 3.67: Class 11 0-6-0 diesel No. 12113 transferred to Royston from Hull Dairycoates.

Summer, 1967: 8F 2-8-0s from Royston still dominate Carlton-Goole freight workings.

2.10.67: With about 20 8Fs still on its books, Royston becomes the West Riding's last steam depot after the withdrawal of the remaining steam allocations at Normanton, Holbeck, and Low Moor.

Above: Photographs of trains on the GC Chapeltown line seem rare but this one makes up for the shortage. J11/3 No. 64373 pilots a B1 up the bank from Grange Lane to Ecclesfield with a 1950s excursion composed mainly of ex-LNER Gresley coaches. *(B.N.Collins)*

Below: On the outskirts of Sheffield, Grange Lane station survived almost intact well into the 1980s. Class 20s Nos. 20130 and 20025 were waiting for the gates to be opened while returning with a load of coke from Smithywood on 29th May, 1979. *(Adrian Booth)*
The signal boxes were still in use at Meadow Hall, Grange Lane and Ecclesfield for absolute block signalling . The top speed was 30mph and there were Up and Down refuge sidings at Grange Lane which closed to passengers on 7th December, 1953 and to goods on 31st December, 1956 .

Above: On 21st September, 1958 the Railway Correspondence and Travel Society's South Yorkshireman No.4 railtour took the GC line to Barnsley. B1 No. 61165 and D11 No. 62660 *Butler Henderson* storm the bank at Ecclesfield while running parallel to the Midland line. *(B.N.Collins)*

Below: It seems the L&Y 2-4-2Ts got everywhere, even on to the Midland. No. 50650 calls at Chapeltown South with the 12.15pm Sheffield Midland to Barnsley Court House on 15th November, 1955. By 1996, a supermarket and car park covered the goods yard(closed 12th July, 1965) while new platforms were built immediately beyond the old ones in 1982. Chapeltown became Chapeltown South in 1951, reverting to Chapeltown when Central closed. *(R.J.Buckley)*

Above: Jubilee No. 45581 *Bihar and Orissa* rolls the Poole-Bradford through Chapeltown South and over the junction with the Thorncliffe ironworks branch on 16th July, 1966. *(P.B.Booth / N.E.Stead collection)*

The 1968 Eastern Region Sectional Appendix stated that the Newton Chambers & Co. sidings, Thorncliffe, were protected by a moveable scotch block normally padlocked across the rail using a key kept in the signal box.

The Thorncliffe works of Newton Chambers was a huge complex mining coal and making iron, steel, coke, bricks, tar and chemicals.

It was connected to the GC line, and to the Midland line which ran into the works and divided into high and low level branches. An internal railway linked coke ovens at Westwood with two collieries

The LMS delivered iron ore from Northamptonshire and limestone from Buxton until 1942 when the blast furnaces were irreparably damaged by measures to reduce glare during wartime blackouts.

Products included large steel fabrications,like bridge sections, and bottled Izal disinfectant. It was dispatched during the 1950s and 60s in block trains of green Izal-liveried pallet vans fitted with internal air bags which were inflated to protect the fragile cargo. Rail traffic, using the low level branch, lasted until 1971.

Below: Manning Wardle 0-6-0ST *Silkstone*, built in Leeds in 1871, was one of several such engines once working on the Newton Chambers system. *(David Green collection)*

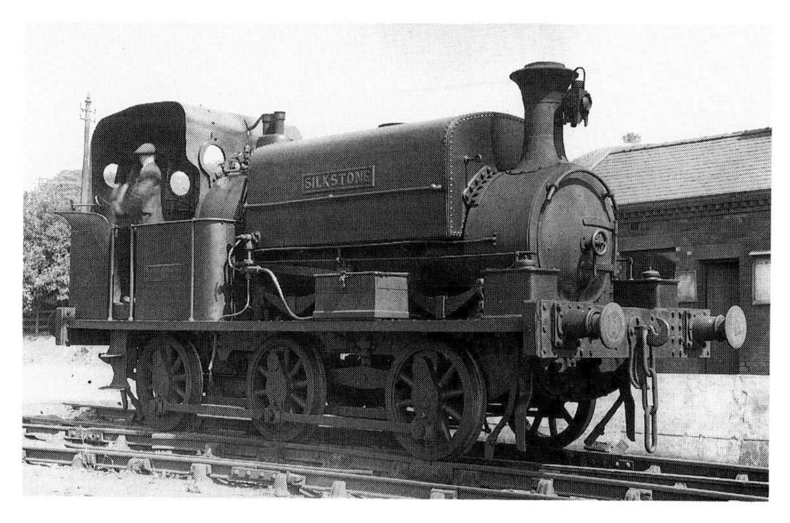

Top: Steam locomotives worked on at collieries and coking works for 15 years after those on BR but diesels, road transport and closures eventually caught up with them
This 0-4-0ST was one of the very last steam engines built by Hudswell Clarke of Leeds when it was completed in 1961 as works No. 1891. It could still be seen in the 1970s from Sheffield-Barnsley trains while working at Skiers Spring Colliery, Wentworth, as on 20th April, 1971. *(Adrian Booth)*

Left: Elsecar & Hoyland station as it was looking towards Barnsley early in the 20th century.
Apart from modern trappings and conversion of the platform buildings to open fronted shelters, it actually looks little different in 1996. The stations on this line were destaffed in 1970. *(Lens of Sutton)*

Right: Wombwell West station looking south on 3rd May, 1960.
Since then the signal box has gone and the platform buildings have been converted to open fronted shelters.
(David Green)
The 1968 ER Sectional Appendix stated that trains could be shunted into a siding to let other trains pass between Wombwell and Skiers Spring. It was operated by a ground frame controlled by a key kept in the frame at Wombwell West signal box.

Top: Ivatt class 2 2-6-0 No. 46499 passes under the GC Chapeltown line at Smithley and approaches Wombwell with the 4.30pm Barnsley Court House to Sheffield Midland in June, 1958. The train includes two empty milk tanks probably from the Co-op dairy at Summer Lane. The Wharncliffe branch comes in from the left alongside the train. *(Peter Sunderland)*

Below: Adding to steam age variety were 'sandwich trains' like this one crossing Monk Spring Junction on its way from Barnsley to Sheffield Midland in June, 1958. The train consisted of push-pull coaches with the tank engine in the middle. *(Peter Sunderland)*

Above: One of Royston's 4Fs makes a spectacular show as it heads on to the Cudworth line at Monk Spring Junction with coal for Carlton yards. The tall overbridge just beyond the junction was still a landmark with its timber piers in 1996. *(Kenneth Field)*

Below: This panoramic view taken on 5th October, 1952 shows Ardsley Sidings signal box and the Monk Spring-Cudworth line in the foreground with the H&B Stairfoot-Cudworth line immediately below. Crossing the bridge beyond the gipsy camp is the Houghton Colliery line and beyond that the embankment carrying the Barnsley-Oakwell curve, the spoil heaps of Barnsley Main Colliery, and Oaks Viaduct carrying the Monk Bretton line. *(David Green)*

The winter 1959/60 working timetable showed the following overnight freights booked to run via Monk Spring and Cudworth: 4.48pm SuX Bristol-Hunslet Lane class C, 10.40pm SuX Leicester-Hunslet class C, 4.45pm Water Orton-Glasgow class C, 9.25pm SO Sheffield Grimesthorpe-Royston light engine, 12.10am MX Stourton-Chaddesden class D, 1.45am MX Carlton South - Leicester class D, and 11.45pm SX Stourton-Sheffield Wicker class F.

Above: The changing scene at Quarry Junction in April, 1960 as work goes on to install the new layout. In the foreground on its new embankment is the line from Mexborough which has been lifted to meet the new connection bringing the Midland line from Chapeltown down from the left. The Barnsley Main colliery sidings are down on the right and the old Midland track bed to Barnsley West Junction and Court House just to the right of the steam crane.The other crane is stood on the Monk Bretton line track bed. *(David Green)*

Below: Looking towards Mexborough at Quarry Junction on 24th April, 1960 with parts of the redundant intersection bridge which carried the Court House line being loaded up. Barnsley Main colliery sidings and brickworks are on the left. *(David Green collection)*

The April, 1960 remodelling of Quarry Junction was carried out in three main stages:-

Stage One - raising Mexborough line, involving demolition of a road bridge and its replacement with a footbridge on a higher level.

Stage Two - connecting the Midland Sheffield line to the Mexborough line at Quarry Jn. Removing bridge carrying the MR line over the Mexborough line, and providing substantial earthworks enabling the two to be linked. Needed full possession of all lines for the whole Easter weekend.

Stage Three -raise Mexborough line to final level. A three quarter-mile stretch lifted by up to 14ft using 150 wagons of ballast a week. Lifted one foot at a time to keep trains running.

The existing Quarry Jn. signal box was in the way of the new junction and had to be replaced by a new one on the site of the old junction.

Barnsley Exchange was given new ticket and parcels offices, improved waiting and staff accommodation and electric lighting. A second, shorter, platform was added on the site of the engine shed, demolished in February.

David Green's earliest memories of the railways in Barnsley were as a young trainspotter tagging along in the early 1950s with older boys on their daily trips to the lineside near Summer Lane station.

"Initially I went along to be 'one of the gang' but I soon began to notice other things besides the numbers painted on the engines.

"My junior school at Keir Street was alongside the railway near Summer Lane and playtimes(and some lesson times) were spent watching for the trains, especially when we could see the signal was "up". One train in particular impressed me for it was composed mainly of coal wagons painted red with the name 'OLD SILKSTONE' in large letters on the sides. I later found that the wagons came not from Silkstone as might be imagined but from Dodworth Colliery just down the line.

"Early evening was spent by Jumble Lane level crossing. Here we could watch trains entering and leaving Court House or 'Top Station', as well as Exchange and the constant movements of engines to and from the engine shed, all accompanied by continuous opening and closing of the crossing gates.

"The main attractions were the two fish trains which passed through each night - one about 7.30pm and the second about 8.30pm. Most engines seen in Barnsley were the same day after day but these trains brought different engines. The first one in particular wassometimes hauled by a 'namer'. The second was the best because it was always double - headed, even if the first engine - the pilot - was a common Barnsley loco. The massive train engine, a K3 2-6-0 with its 6ft diameter boiler was something else. This train always stopped at Jumble Lane for the K3 to take water and the crossing gates were closed for some time as a result.

"This gave us time to rush through the bus station and round to the far end of Exchange to watch the 'sparks' as the long and heavy train of fish vans tried to build up speed for the 1 in 41 - 50 climb up to Summer Lane.

"Standing on the platform end at Summer Lane one evening, I heard this train set off from Jumble Lane and listened to the increasing noise as it passed through Barnsley and up the steep gradient. The sight and sound as it passed was awesome - a sensation immediately followed by the overpowering smell from several hundred tons of Manchester-bound fish!

"I soon realised that trainspotting in Barnsley would be a most frustrating hobby because the same engines appeared time after time. Stories of different and better attractions nearby at Cudworth and even Stairfoot proved irresistible.

"A keen cyclist, I set off to explore different parts. Cudworth was especially rewarding with real expresses going through at speed hauled by green engines with names.

"My Box Brownie camera was very useful for recording views which are now history.

"I began to combine my interests in railways and photography and also developed an interest in the history of the railways around Barnsley. Mind you, I still found it hard to resist summer Saturday visits to Doncaster to watch the 'Streaks' on the main line.

" Sadly, most of the railways in the Barnsley area have vanished along with the industry they served. And so too have the spotters."

New Oaks Junction looking east. This was where the GC Sheffield line went off right from the Mexborough line which went straight on. For good measure a tramway passed under the railway from the flooded Stairfoot brickworks claypit on the right. No railway remains today. *(David Green)*

STAIRFOOT & THE COAL RAILWAY

Top: Looking towards Barnsley in the 1950s from a footbridge at New Oaks Junction. On the left are Stairfoot sidings with the Yorkshire Tar Distillers Oaks by-products works on the right. *(David Green)*

Centre: Stairfoot No. 2 box in a non too scenic setting, opposite the tar works, seen from Wombwell Lane on 14th October, 1952. *(David Green)*

Bottom: Stairfoot station looking towards Barnsley in the early 1900s.
Opened in 1871 to replace Ardsley station further east, it closed to passengers on 16th September, 1957 and to goods on 16th December, 1963. The Barnsley - Mexborough line itself continued to carry freight until the 1980s. *(Lens of Sutton)*

Above: Stairfoot Junction was the western extremity of the Hull and Barnsley Railwayand that is it coming in from Cudworth in the left foreground. B1 No. 61165 and now preserved D11 4-4-0 No. 62660 *Butler Henderson* visit the already closed station while on the Barnsley line with the RCTS South Yorkshireman No.4 railtour of 21st September, 1958. *(N.E.Stead collection)*

A section of railway remained at Stairfoot until 1983 to serve the Beatson Clarke glassworks where a yellow Hibberd diesel shunted sand wagons from BR. It pushed them one at a time up an inclined gantry into a tipping shed. Old capstains remained from a time when it might have been rope-worked.

Below: Looking towards Barnsley from Stairfoot station footbridge with N5 0-6-2T No. 69367 on pilot duty during the 1950s. The Monk Spring-Cudworth portion of the Midland's Chapeltown Loop goes over the top and the H&B line heads off to the right. The viaduct was demolished bit by bit in 1966. *(David Green)*

Above: An idyllic view of the flimsy looking signal box at Stairfoot North Junction in the 1950s. Original GC class 04/1 2-8-0 No. 63625 simmers behind, on the Houghton branch, while the Barnsley Coal Railway runs in front. *(David Green)*

Below: O4/3 2-8-0 No. 63656 brings a load of coal down from Houghton and is about to pass under the Monk Spring-Cudworth line at Ardsley on 10th July, 1954. *(The late T. S. Walker)*

Top: N5 0-6-2T No. 69320 hauls the pick-up from Nostell along the Stairfoot line past Oakwell Junction in 1955. *(P.J.Lynch)*

Centre: Old Oaks Junction and its 'garden shed' signal box in 1952. The curve to Oakwell Junction sweeps away left while the Mexborough line goes across the front. *(David Green)*

Bottom: Oakwell Junction in the late 1950s. The maltings branch goes to the right, the Stairfoot line straight ahead, the curve to Old Oaks Junction to the left, andOaks Viaduct dominates the skyline. *(David Green)*

The winter 1959/60 freight timetable showed 15 booked freights each way a day on the Barnsley Coal Railway round the clock, plus engine and brake van movements.

They included the 11.10pm Ardsley to Mottram and 6.24pm Woodford Halse-Ardsley class Ds; class H trains between Ardsley and Mottram or Annesley an 8pm Thursdays class H from Northwich to Wrenthorpe, a 2.10am Dewsnap-Leeds Wellington St. class E, a 6.45pm Workington to Wath class J, an overnight class J from Liverpool Brunswick to Wharncliffe Woodmoor, 1.12 and 3.40pm mineral trains from Moorhouse sidings to Mottram, and local trips including the 2.30pm class K Stairfoot to Oakwell and back.

Above: Coal Railway stations early in the 20th century - Staincross for Mapplewell(top), and Notton & Royston(above)on the embankment which divided the two villages. Both closed to passengers on 22nd September, 1930 and Notton to goods on 2nd January, 1961. (*Both Lens of Sutton*)

Below: Now preserved O4/1 2-8-0 No. 63601 hauls a loaded coal train southbound past Old Mill Lane goods yard and signal box in April, 1961. The depot handled everything from general goods, coal and petroleum to vegetables and potatoes but closed on 30th March,1959. *(Gordon Coltas)*

Above: Wintersett & Ryhill on 7th June, 1953 with D11 4-4-0 No. 62667 *Somme* calling while on an RCTS special. This station was just Ryhill until 1927 and just Wintersett from 1951. (*B.K.B.Green*)

On arrival at the...Wharncliffe Woodmoor colliery end of the One Engine in Steam line, drivers must sound whistle and if permission not received from the NCB shunter to enter the sidings, the guard must proceed to colliery weigh office...*Eastern Region Appendix, 1968*

Above: Viewed from the footbridge, Wintersett as it was, looking towards Nostell, on 4th August, 1960.
(H.B. Priestley / Howard Turner collection)

Down trains must stop when clear of the points operated from Wharncliffe Woodmoor ground frame, and before descending the incline, the brakes of each alternative wagon must be applied. If worked by a tender locomotive and under half a load, it may, after stopping, proceed without any brakes applied...Trains must stop at Smithies to release brakes. *Eastern Region Sectional Appendix, 1968.*

SHORT MEMORIES

4.11..67: Royston 8F 48276 works the last Eastern Region steam duty, the 15.00 Carlton-Goole. It returns light to Royston where it is withdrawn

23.12.68: Flooding on the Worsborough line causes freight trains, complete with class 76 electric locos, to be diesel-hauled through Barnsley. Two diesels are needed on the front and one on the rear for the climb up to West Silkstone.

Spring, 1982: Hunslet 0-6-0ST No. 3183, the last NCB Barnsley Area steam loco, leaves Woolley Colliery for preservation.

COAL & INDUSTRY

Coking works are impressive if not pretty places - huge plants belching smoke, steam and fire.

They usually mean railway activity of some sort , bringing coal in and taking coke away.

Coke is made by heating coal to 1,300 degrees Centigrade, releasing impurities and creating by-products like tar, ammonia and gas. What remains is 99 per cent carbon.

When ready the coke is dropped red hot into a long side-hopper wagon running on a track alongside the ovens, and taken to be quenched before loading into conventional rail wagons, lorries or stockpiling.

Special electric locomotives, collecting current from a side wire, work the coke car but conventional locos can be used if needed.

As Barnsley coal was good for coking there were several large plants in the area. Today, only the Monckton plant is still in production, but with no conventional locomotives and very infrequent rail traffic to use its sidings which still connect to the former Midland main line at Royston Junction.

Above: This strange machine was an electric locomotive. Its purpose was to pull the special car which collected freshly made hot coke from the coke ovens and was a type well used around Barnsley. This one, built by Greenwood and Batley of Leeds in 1955, was at Smithywood.

Below: A general view of Monckton coke works, Royston, with two coke car locos present, on 10thApril, 1980. In 1996 this was the only place left in the area where a coke car loco could still be seen at work. *(Both Adrian Booth)*

Above: Making a brief distraction from the hustle and bustle of the main line railway, Peckett 0-6-0ST *Salisbury* shunts Wharncliffe Woodmoor No. 4 & 5 Colliery (Carlton Main) on 23rd July, 1962. Scores of little tank engines like this once worked the NCB lines and sidings around Barnsley. *(Peter Rose)*

Right: This Sentinel steam locomotive was shunting at Barnsley Main in 1964. Based on a steam lorry, it had a vertical boiler and chain drive with gears. *(Christopher Davison)*

Left: The huge Grimethorpe Coalite Fuel and Chemical works forms a backdrop for ex-BR Drewry 0-6-0 diesel No. D2284, still in BR green while stood outside its new engine shed in 1976.
The picture was taken from a BR civil engineers' inspection unit on the Dearne Valley line.
(Stephen Chapman)

October, 1969: NCB 0-4-0ST 1893/61, the last steam loco built by Leeds firm Hudswell Clarke is withdrawn from regular service at Barrow Colliery but remains in reserve to a diesel. As well as internal shunting, Barrow locomotives made four trips a day with coal over the connecting branch to Dovecliffe, on the GC Barnsley-Sheffield line.

Above: Hunslet-built Austerity 0-6-0ST *Monckton No.1* (works No. 3788, built 1953) makes a powerful impression outside the engine shed at North Gawber Colliery on 10th June, 1975. Alas, it was by then playing second fiddle to a diesel while Hudswell Clarke 0-6-0T No. 1857/ 1952 behind it was out of use. No. 3788, equivelant to BR class 4F, saw use again in autumn, 1976 but left the pit for preservation in February, 1980. The rail system was abandoned by 1985.

Below: A new shaft with a railway appeared after the 1980s centralisation of coal winding on three big pits. It was called Redbrook Colliery, Barnsley, and this little 1978-built Hunslet diesel, seen on 30th November, 1985, was used on the 2ft 3in gauge railway for moving materials about the site. There was no standard gauge. *(Both Adrian Booth)*

In 1973, the NCB still had 12 steam locos at five collieries in its Barnsley Area. 0-6-0ST HE2857/43 and 0-4-0STs HC1889 and 1890/60 at Dodworth; 0-6-0STs HE3183/44, WB2753/44 and HE3208/45 at Woolley, 0-6-0STs HE3212/45 and HE3788/53 at North Gawber along with 0-6-0T HC1857/52; 0-4-0STs 1891 and 1892/60 at Skiers Spring and 1893/61 at Barrow. In addition, 0-6-0STs HE3192 and 3193/44 were at the Smithywood coking plant. HE3192 was the last steam loco in the area, working until 1984 and leaving in 1986 for preservation at the South Yorkshire Railway, Meadow Hall.

Top: Steam-hauled coke trains still ran alongside the GC Chapeltown line into the 1980s - at least through Smithywood coking works sidings. On 7th September, 1978, Hunslet 0-6-0ST SWCP 1 (works No. 3192) was pulling BR 21 ton hoppers over the weighbridge. National Smokeless Fuels locos like this one were blue and NCB Barnsley Area engines green. *(Stephen Chapman)*

Centre: Ex-BR class 03 0-6-0 No. D2199 among the pithead gear at Rockingham Colliery on 27th March, 1978. Between 1977 and 1983 this well travelled loco was at Rockingham, Barrow, Houghton Main, Royston Drift, back to Barrow and then Royston again.

Bottom: Locally-built by Thomas Hill of Kilnhurst, Rotherham in 1964, this diesel was active at Smithywood colliery on 4th June, 1971. *(Both Adrian Booth)*